EXEMPLARY CLASSROOM QUESTIONING

Practices to Promote Thinking and Learning

Marie Menna Pagliaro

ROWMAN & LITTLEFIELD EDUCATION

A division of
ROWMAN & LITTLEFIELD PUBLISHERS, INC.
Lanham • New York • Toronto • Plymouth, UK

Published by Rowman & Littlefield Education
A division of Rowman & Littlefield Publishers, Inc.
A wholly owned subsidary of The Rowman & Littlefield Publishing Group, Inc.
4501 Forbes Boulevard, Suite 200, Lanham, Maryland 20706
http://www.rowmaneducation.com

Estover Road, Plymouth PL6 7PY, United Kingdom

British Library Cataloguing in Publication Information Available

Library of Congress Cataloging-in-Publication Data
Pagliaro, Marie Menna, 1934-
    Exemplary classroom questioning : practices to promote thinking and
learning / Marie Menna Pagliaro.
        p. cm.
    Includes bibliographical references.
    ISBN 978-1-61048-456-5 (cloth : alk. paper) — ISBN 978-1-61048-457-2
(pbk. : alk. paper) — ISBN 978-1-61048-458-9 (ebook)
    1. Inquiry-based learning. 2. Active learning. 3. Thought and thinking—
Study and teaching. I. Title.
    LB1027.23.P35 2011
        370.15'2—dc22
                                                            2011015723

CONTENTS

TABLES

FIGURES

INTRODUCTION

Researchers have consistently reported that questioning is one of the teaching skills that has the greatest effect on student achievement (Wang et al., 1993; Interstate New Teacher Assessment and Support Consortium [INTASC], 1995; Good, 1996; Danielson, 1996, 2008). Therefore, considerable attention should be given to developing the questioning skills of both novice and veteran teachers.

At the core of all learning is the ability to ask questions. Although classroom questioning originally focused on having students acquire specific knowledge, more recently there has been a shift toward using questions to promote and enhance learning. In addition to learning academic subjects, students must learn to deal with an ever-changing world by using questions to handle their own lives analytically and intelligently.

Treffinger (2008) challenges teachers to reflect on the current everyday experiences of children and teenagers. They can communicate through images, by watching videos, or by simply speaking with young people all over the world. Our students have access to more technology than that in the workplaces of their parents two decades ago.

Currently, students are studying new subjects that did not exist 10 years ago and will prepare for careers that are not in existence today.

It is becoming increasingly common for our students to interact with people of diverse backgrounds and collaborate with people all over the planet. With all of these factors to deal with and with increasing unknown elements in the world, students will need the tools to become effective, creative, and critical thinkers. And for these kinds of thinking skills, questioning is an essential tool.

Questioning is fundamental to investigating systematically all curriculum areas. In the pursuit of this investigation, students must question the reason for the inquiry, make use of questions to guide the search for information, integrate the results, and employ questions to evaluate these results.

Teachers play a critical role in questioning. It is therefore incumbent upon them to plan questions very carefully so that student knowledge and comprehension will be enhanced. The quality of the question determines the depth of student understanding. Moreover, teachers are models in the questioning process for their students. Therefore, the high quality of a teacher's questioning should facilitate the student's ability to ask questions and think independently.

Chapter 1 provides the foundation for successful questioning by describing how to establish a supportive environment in which all class members feel comfortable and willing to participate.

Chapter 2 reviews productive reasons for asking questions as well as reasons when asking questions would not be constructive.

In order to examine the way teachers word questions, deliver questions, and subsequently react to students' responses, a framework for analyzing these dynamics is introduced in chapter 3. This chapter then analyzes the first part of the framework by offering effective ways that teachers should construct questions and address them to the students.

Chapter 4 describes teacher-questioning practices during framing and immediately after the original question is posed that actually interfere with the learning process and with effective student–teacher interaction.

Chapter 5 describes how teachers can most productively respond to students' answers to promote greater class participation and deeper understanding.

To help clarify the ways that teachers, through their reactions to student responses, can impede student participation and achievement, chapter 6 provides some behaviors that teachers display that can inadvertently contribute to this negative result.

Traditionally, it was the teacher's role to do all or most of the questioning. Chapter 7 presents many activities to involve students in the question-asking process and give them ownership of learning.

Different types of questions elicit different types of mental activities from students. Chapter 8 reviews several taxonomies teachers can use to structure questions that will involve students in higher mental processes.

Chapter 9 goes deeper into the question-framing process by examining what critical thinkers do, what critical thinking is not, and the difference between problem solving and critical thinking. This chapter further explores how the brain is involved in thinking and what teachers can do with this knowledge to improve their students' thinking. A framework for promoting critical thinking in lessons is presented along with abridged lessons in different subjects and grade levels that demonstrate how to use objectives in the framework to transform traditional lessons into those that enhance critical thinking.

Chapter 10 provides a structure for using Socratic (dialectic) questioning in the classroom and a mini-script and full script illustrating how this type of questioning can be used. Differing opinions are presented regarding the use of Socratic questioning.

Chapter 11 explores types of information we are constantly bombarded with and how we can critically question this information to determine what is valid and what is not.

Because knowledge of questioning skills reaches its maximum value when this knowledge is actually implemented, chapter 12 shows how coaching rubrics can be used to make the transition from knowledge to performance. This chapter also provides a rationale for employing coaching rubrics and instructions regarding how they are used to assess and improve teacher performance.

Throughout the book, there are numerous actual questioning examples relevant to both elementary and secondary students/teachers. Teachers are busy people, so examples are provided clearly and succinctly. There are also classroom clips and classroom scripts. With the exception of references to seminal and foundational works upon which practice has been built and expanded, much of the supportive research provided is from the past decade.

Periodically, differing opinions about questioning are offered by educators. When this situation occurs, the varying views are presented for consideration.

Self-reflection questions are provided at the end of each chapter. Through this reflection, teachers will master the content of this book and become more aware of the potential they have through their questioning skills to increase not only their students' academic achievement but also their quality of life. An extra bonus will be noted when the effective questioning developed as a result of implementing the information in this book leads to fewer classroom behavior problems.

Marie Menna Pagliaro

(1)

ESTABLISHING AN EFFECTIVE ENVIRONMENT FOR QUESTIONING

Before embarking on a discussion of questioning, it must be emphasized that all questions involve content. The teacher must master the content if he or she is to develop an environment for effective questioning skills. The more a teacher knows about content, the better the questions the teacher has the potential to ask—especially those questions that lead students to deeper meaning and critical thinking.

Consider, for example, the financial crisis that hit the United States in late September of 2008. A teacher who knows about economics, regulation, oversight, banking, history, and markets would be well equipped to ask relevant important questions. Some of these might be:

"What does this crisis involve?"
"What series of events led to this crisis?"
"Who are the players?"
"What were their responsibilities?"
"Which past signals could have alerted us to this problem?"
"How could we ensure that this will not happen again?"
"Which uncertainties lie ahead?"
"What conditions would have to occur to be able to pay back the American people?"

When analyzing questioning, it is useful to point out that there is a distinction between the skill of formulating the original question itself and its interactive skill, which involves the delivery of the question by the teacher and his or her reaction to its response from the student. A teacher may have an excellent idea for a question but may not phrase or distribute it well or handle appropriately an answer a student may give. Therefore, the question itself loses its effectiveness. In addition, the vocabulary the teacher uses in questions must be consistent with the vocabulary parameters of the students.

Questions do not occur in isolation. For both teacher and student questioning to be effective, it must be implemented in a supportive learning environment. In this environment, the teacher is a facilitator who fosters not only students' academic growth but also their personal and social growth.

The classroom is a learning community in which there is shared responsibility for the success of all community members. The teacher's role is one of a guide and coach as opposed to a person who pours information into students' heads. There is a warm friendly atmosphere in the classroom, where all members show mutual respect for and support each other in a spirit of cooperation in which all have a stake in the success of all other members. This atmosphere produces a *comfort level* in which students are more willing to take risks in answering and asking questions to enhance achievement.

Recently, several characteristics have been demonstrated to be conducive to promoting a positive emotional classroom environment for questioning: having a caring attitude, setting high standards, and having *all* classroom members—including the teacher—show mutual respect and support for each other (Oakes & Lipton, 2003). In short, there is a sense of community in the class when all classroom members are connected with one another.

Research has indicated that rapport with the teacher and fellow classmates made students feel connected and willing to participate, thus enhancing cognitive and affective learning (Frisby & Martin, 2010). This supportive learning environment welcomes student questions, is nonjudgmental, fosters the attitude that it is all right to make mistakes because we all do and we learn from them, and does not allow students to be subjected to ridicule from anyone in the learning community. Students are given the time to think and are challenged at their appropriate levels.

The seating arrangement in the classroom is critically important for effective questioning. Whenever possible, students should sit in a circle where they all face each other and can address each other in a more personal way. In this setting, all students are easily visible to the teacher and to each other with little opportunity for students to conduct unrelated activities. The teacher is free to move around more easily, thus giving her contact with everyone in the class.

In a supportive learning environment, the teacher is enthusiastic and plans a dynamic curriculum. He expects all to participate by framing questions thoughtfully and by assisting (with the help of the rest of the class) any student who does not know an answer or who does not complete a full response.

Once you have established this supportive learning environment with your students, you will be well on your way to implementing questioning (and your entire curriculum) more effectively.

CHARACTERISTICS OF AN EFFECTIVE QUESTIONING ENVIRONMENT

Teacher knowledgeable in subject matter
Teacher as a facilitator
Mutual caring
Mutual respect
Mutual support
Shared responsibility for success of all
Success of one critical to success of all
Feeling of connectedness
Nonjudgmental attitude
High comfort level

SELF-REFLECTION

- Why are the characteristics of an effective questioning environment important for questioning?
- Which of these characteristics are currently reflected in your classroom?

(2)

REASONS FOR ASKING
(AND NOT ASKING) QUESTIONS

Read the following two sentences. After you read them, think of how you reacted mentally to each.

The author of "To His Coy Mistress" is Andrew Marvell.

How does Marvell use imagery in this poem to convey his message?

The first is a declarative sentence, a statement that *tells* you something. If you were paying attention, you absorbed or received the information. The second sentence is a question that requires you to *respond*. You are more actively involved mentally when asked a question, especially if the question is framed in a way that allows you to respond through high-level thinking. Thus, the proper type of questioning is extremely important in order to engage students in learning and in promoting high-level thinking and problem solving.

From your own school experience, you might recall that most classroom time is spent in verbal interaction (questioning), largely between teachers and students. In fact, researchers have reported that questioning is the second most common method used in instruction after lecturing (Black, 2001).

You might be surprised to learn that of this verbal interaction, 80 percent involves questions by teachers and answers by students, and that teachers, both elementary and secondary, ask as many as 100 questions per hour (Borich, 2007). Similar results are reported by Vogler (2008), with teachers asking 300–400 questions per day and up to 120 questions per hour.

Since so much classroom time is devoted to questioning, and research has identified a strong correlation between effective questioning skills and student test performance (Cotton, 2000; Marzano et al., 2001), it is vital that questioning be implemented well. Questioning is an essential learning tool and one of the most complex skills for teachers—even experienced teachers—to master. To add to the complexity, different types of questions are appropriate for different types of instructional strategies.

Though it is difficult even for veteran teachers to demonstrate excellent questioning skills, it is important that you *practice* doing so because student achievement is at stake. Once you master these skills, you will immediately notice a positive difference in your students, a smoother flow of interactions, and more dynamic relationships in your classroom. You will even notice fewer discipline problems.

WAYS QUESTIONS ARE USED IN THE CLASSROOM

Before you can enhance the quality of your questioning formulation and interactive techniques, it would be helpful for you to first distinguish among the various ways questions are used in classrooms. There are several appropriate reasons for asking questions. These reasons are:

1. To elicit information even though the question is posed as a statement. Examples:

   "Hold up your 'Yes' card if 4 + 3 equals 8 or your "No" card if it does not." This statement is actually asking the students, "How many of you agree with the conclusion?"

   "Contrast the examples with the nonexamples." This statement is asking, "How are the examples different from the nonexamples?"

2. To capture the students' interest, motivate them, and engage students in learning a unit or lesson. Examples:

"What do you think it would be like if you walked through a forest and met some dinosaurs?"

"What concerns would come to mind if you learned that gasoline was going to be rationed?"

3. To facilitate classroom management. Examples:

"Whose turn is it to take the attendance?"
"Do you have a late pass?"

4. To meet the affective needs of students. Examples:

"How would you feel if our hero, Bill, had done to you what he did to Fred?"
"What would make this subject more interesting for you?"

5. As an assessment device *before* instruction to determine if students have the prerequisite knowledge on a topic to begin new instruction. Example: Before beginning division, you would want to ascertain if the students had mastered basic multiplication facts by asking questions such as

"How much is 8×4?"
"How much is 7×8?"

6. As an assessment device *during* instruction to determine whether or not to proceed with instruction or go back and reteach the objective in a different way. Examples:

"Before we continue, who can summarize the first three steps in solving this word problem?"
"What are the main issues that have been addressed in this chapter so far?"

7. As an evaluative device at the *end* of a unit or lesson to determine whether or not unit goals or lesson objectives have been achieved. Examples:

"How did our victory in World War II affect the development of our country?"
"What kind of diet would you plan to ensure that you will maintain optimal health and weight?"

8. To promote inquiring minds. Examples:

   "How would you rearrange the events in the story so that Alana would not have to die?"
   "Assuming that the terrorists were victorious, how would Europe and the United States be affected?"

9. To promote critical thinking. Examples:

   "What evidence would you need to support this position?"
   "How would you verify this information?"

10. To summarize lessons and review previously learned material. Examples:

    "What steps do we have to follow to solve quadratic equations?
    "Yesterday we discussed characterization. How did the author represent Kathy as a character in the novel?

11. To stimulate students to pursue information independently. Examples:

    "Now that we have completed this unit on weather, what other information can you find to help predict what kind of hurricane season we will have?"
    "What other projects can you explore to attract tourists to California?"

12. To provide a mental set for the learning experience *before* the learning actually takes place. For example, in a lesson on units, the teacher identifies the *organizing (big) ideas* and *essential questions* that the unit will address. Essential questions serve as an umbrella for the unit. As such, they guide activities, assignments, and assessments that are designed to assist students in answering the essential questions.

    Essential questions are arguable, relevant to students' lives, student-friendly, and focus on *deeper* meanings, not the type that are answerable in a word or sentence (Udelhofen, 2006). Some examples of essential questions are:

    "How does what we eat affect our health?"
    "How did the culture of the North and South contribute to the causes of the Civil War?"

Nonexamples of essential questions are:

"Which foods contain calcium?"
"What battles did the Union win?"

During lessons, the teacher uses questions to make students aware of a particular objective or set of objectives.

"Before you read this story, I want you to pay particular attention to why Ashley got into trouble and what she first thought she might do about it."

13. To develop insights that allow students to see new relationships. Example:

"How would you compare the problem that Jessica had in the story to the situation that is currently occurring with the mayor in our town?"

14. To develop deeper insights into a topic. With brain research indicating that it is more important to process information in depth, rather than breadth (Jensen, 1998), questions should lead to acquiring a more complete understanding of what is being studied. Examples:

"To better understand how we arrived at this government bailout decision, what additional information would we need?"
"How could we get this information?"

REASONS FOR NOT ASKING QUESTIONS

Equally important as the reasons for asking questions are the reasons for not asking questions of students. Reasons for not asking questions include:

1. Calling on students when they are misbehaving, thus giving them the attention they may be deliberately seeking. (However, calling on a student who is not paying attention or misbehaving in other ways may be a subtle way to remind that student to participate positively, if misbehaving is not chronic with that particular student. This reminder should be employed in a nonthreatening way.)

2. Alerting students that they may be asked to answer questions solely as a device to control behavior problems as opposed to the development of quality thinking and learning.
3. Involving students with over-questioning that does not promote their cognitive development but just keeps the entire class answering. The teacher may also attempt to involve students by asking questions to achieve lesson objectives when other techniques would be more productive.
4. Communicating the idea that the teacher is the source of all information rather than a copartner and colearner with students in a process that finds answers to important questions.
5. Asserting the teacher's role as *the* question asker, thus minimizing the same important role in the student.
6. Embarrassing students by deliberately asking questions to which they could not know the answers.

SELF-REFLECTION

- From the list of reasons for asking questions, which do you consider to be the most important? Why?
- Are there any other reasons for asking questions you would add to this list?
- Do you agree with the reasons for *not* asking questions? If not, with which reasons do you disagree? Why? What other reasons would you consider to be nonproductive?

(3)

EFFECTIVE QUESTIONING PRACTICES WHEN FRAMING AND DELIVERING QUESTIONS

Though many reasons for asking questions were explained in chapter 2, the most important reason for studying questioning skills is to learn how to actively involve your students in acquiring, exploring, and manipulating meaningful information (Weiss & Pasley, 2004). This type of questioning creates a powerful learning environment.

Many questions are asked before a unit or lesson, at the end of lessons, and at the end of units. However, the opportunity for asking skillful questions occurs most frequently in lessons involving discussions, recitations, reviews, or demonstrations, whether the questioning is conducted with the whole class, small groups, or during individualized instruction.

Regardless of which grouping method is used, this questioning usually follows a series of phases (Dillon, 1988). These phases serve as a framework for analyzing effective and ineffective questioning practices in this chapter and in the following three chapters.

After structuring a topic with a statement,

- Phase 1. The teacher frames a question and delivers it to one or more students.
- Phase 2. The student(s) provide(s) a response.
- Phase 3. The teacher reacts to that response.

Only Phases 1 and 3 involve teacher behavior.

In the following section, you will examine each of these two phases separately to review which teacher questioning behaviors implemented or avoided will have the most positive effects on students. As you read, consider whether the teacher behavior is concerned with the quality of the question itself or with the delivery. Regardless of the ways questions are framed, delivered, or reacted to, a teacher who proceeds through all phases with interest, enthusiasm, and a conversational tone is highly like to get these same characteristics from students.

PHASE 1: THE TEACHER ASKS A QUESTION AND ADDRESSES IT TO ONE OR MORE STUDENTS

A. Secure the Attention of the Class before Asking a Question

Before asking a question, make sure you have everyone's attention. If students are not listening or not paying attention, then why ask a question or conduct any kind of instruction? Brain research tell us that attention is necessary for memory, and therefore to all learning (Jensen, 1998).

When asking questions, some teachers talk above students' voices. This teacher behavior conveys a subtle message that the question (or lesson) is unimportant and, therefore, not worthy of the students' attention.

B. Try to Keep Lower-Level Questions to a Minimum

Imagine that you are in two different classrooms, one with questions led by Mr. Quinn, the other by Mr. Clark. First read Mr. Quinn's questions and answer his; then read Mr. Clark's and answer his.

Mr. Quinn	Mr. Clark
Where did Columbus first land?	How would you contrast the trip Columbus took with a trip across the ocean today?
How old was Columbus when he came to America?	
When did Columbus discover America?	How would America be now if it remained undiscovered?

Who funded his trip?

What was the name of the ship on which Columbus sailed?

Why did Columbus undertake his expedition?

What would you change if you were making Columbus's trip today?

How is Europe different today as a result of the discovery of the new world?

What are the differences you noticed in *your* responses to the two sets of questions? Try to visualize the scene in these two classrooms and describe what you see before you continue reading.

You probably noted that Mr. Quinn's questions led to one word or short answers. The information elicited required facts or simple memory. The teacher is doing most of the talking in the questioning session.

Ever since the first reported study on questioning was conducted (Stevens, 1912), it has been noted that a vast majority of questions asked by teachers are low level (Wragg, 1993; Wilen, 2001; Wragg & Brown, 2001). Moreover, these low-level questions are predominantly asked from the elementary school through the university levels (Albergaria-Almeida, 2010).

Mr. Quinn's questions are referred to in the educational literature as fact, closed, or *convergent* questions. They lead to simple recall, limited responses, and are usually either right or wrong.

Because this type of question is at the memory level, however, does not mean it is unnecessary or unimportant. Memory matters and is a crucial foundation for all learning and higher thinking levels. Memory (lower cognitive) questions become problematic when they are a vast majority of the questions asked, especially with students whose developmental stage makes it possible for them to learn and grow at a higher level.

Research indicates that lower cognitive questions are more effective with young children when the purpose is the mastery of basic skills. Higher cognitive questions yield superior learning gains for older primary, middle, and secondary students (Gall et al., 2003).

In contrast with the questions of Mr. Quinn, the questions asked by Mr. Clark require longer responses from students. His questions ask students to manipulate facts and use higher levels of thinking. The students do more of the talking and the teacher eventually ends up asking *fewer* questions (Chuska, 1995). Whoever is doing the talking is doing the work, and whoever is doing the work is doing the learning (Wong, 1989). When the quality of the teacher's question elicits a higher cognitive response from the student, student talk is increased.

Mr. Clark's questions are referred to in the educational literature as thought, *divergent*, or open questions. They lead to higher-level thinking and longer responses, and can have several correct answers.

Thought-provoking questions make instruction more student centered. Research is conflicting regarding whether the use of divergent questions actually leads to higher-level thinking (Slavin, 1997; Eggen & Kauchak, 1999), but there is some historical evidence that asking questions that provoke higher-level thinking results in higher achievement (Hunkins, 1974; Redfield & Rousseau, 1981; Wilen & Clegg, 1986; Barden, 1995; Stronge, 2002).

You should be aware of the fact that questions beginning with who, when, and where are generally fact questions. Questions beginning with how, why, or what may be either fact or thought questions, depending upon what follows. Look back at Mr. Quinn's and Mr. Clark's questions and contrast what content follows the "how," "why," and "what" in both lists to determine which questions are fact and which are thought.

Sample questions that elicit divergent and higher-level responses include:

Assuming that . . . what would . . .
Compare the events . . .
Suppose . . .
If . . . then . . .
Predict . . .
Create a situation where . . .
What are some of the possible consequences . . .
Imagine . . .
Which ideas . . .
Contrast the conditions . . .
How might . . .
To what extent would . . .

C. Phrase Questions for Clarity

Consider the following question: "What about Cuba?"

Your reaction probably is "Well, what about it?" You do not have a clear idea regarding what information is being asked. Now consider the question rephrased. "How is the climate of Cuba related to its economy?" This second question gives you a focus and helps you retrieve and coordinate the information needed to respond.

Another type of vague question is "Tell us about triangles." What are you being asked about triangles?

To ensure that questions are clear, they should be narrowed down and not so wordy that students lose track of the information requested. Key questions should be related to the lesson objective and planned in advance to provide clarity so that there is no need to rephrase questions during the lesson.

Writing key questions to which you can refer helps both beginning and experienced teachers keep the lesson on target. Even the most seasoned TV talk show hosts use written questions cued on cards, teleprompters, or laptops. These hosts rehearse the questions before interviewing guests and refer to the questions during the interviews. You can sometimes notice the host's eyes glancing to cues that are invisible to the audience.

After you write your questions, read them *out loud*. Actually hearing them will give you a better handle on how they are coming across. If necessary, adjust the questions. Then, based on the original question, consider possible additional questions that would lead students to deeper understanding of the concepts presented and promote further investigation.

D. Develop Key Questions Sequentially

Set the stage by asking beginning questions with elementary or known content. Subsequent pivotal questions should be planned carefully, presented logically, and asked in sequential order. Planning, writing, and asking questions in sequence also assist students in developing a deeper understanding of information and the opportunity to apply it. Examine once again Mr. Quinn's questions. Think of how you can improve *both* the sequence and the cognitive level.

It is crucial to point out that much can occur spontaneously or serendipitously in the classroom; there may be occasions when pursuing the unexpected instead of what was planned may lead to clarification and deeper knowledge and understanding. This principle holds true for planned lessons as well as for planned questions.

E. Keep the Speed of Your Question Appropriate to Your Students

Recent research has reported that adults speak at an average rate of 170 words per minute (Tobias, 2008). It takes students a longer time to process questions and information in general, with the average 5- to 7-year-old processing speech at the rate of only 120 words per minute and the average student in high school processing speech at the rate of 140–145 words per minute. In *both* cases, the processing rate is considerably less than that of the speaking rate of adults. Therefore, if you want students to listen so that they really hear and understand, speak at a rate that is compatible with their processing level.

F. Increase Wait Time

A common teacher practice in many classrooms is that of rapid-fire questioning. In this type of classroom, the teacher asks a question, immediately calls on a student for a response, immediately reacts to the student's response, and immediately asks another question, thus repeating the same cycle. Though waiting long enough for a student to respond seems to be a relatively simple behavior, *it is one that teachers have difficulty putting into practice*. In general, teachers have little tolerance for silence and may even feel that when there is silence in the classroom, they are losing control.

Rowe (1974) trained teachers to increase time after soliciting a question from students, which she calls *wait-time 1*, by pausing from 3 to 5 seconds. She found that when teachers waited this amount of time, student responses improved in the following ways:

1. The length of the response increases.
2. The number of unsolicited but appropriate responses increases.
3. Failure to respond decreases.
4. Confidence, as reflected in decrease of inflected (question-like tones of voice) responses, increases.
5. Incidence of speculative responses increases.
6. Incidence of child–child comparisons of data increases.
7. Incidence of evidence–inference statements increases.
8. The incidence of student questions increases.

9. Incidence of responses from students rated by teachers as relatively slow increases.
10. The variety in types of moves made by students increases (Rowe, 1974, p. 81).

Rowe (1986) subsequently reported that pausing (increasing wait-time 1) changed the discussion from an "inquisitional" nature where *teachers* do most of the structuring and soliciting, and students do the responding, to a more conversational nature where both the teacher and the students engage in structuring, soliciting, and responding.

To improve the responses of your pupils, you should pause at least 3–5 seconds after asking a question and selecting a student to answer. If after asking questions, you find yourself not pausing long enough before calling on respondents and subsequently decide to increase your wait time, it would be productive to prepare the respondents by informing them of your intent and the reasons for it. Your students will also have to adjust to your new behavior.

G. Ask Only One Question at a Time

What is your reaction to the question, "Where is the liver and what does it do for your body?" You probably do not know which part of the question to think about or answer first. This type of question is often labeled a double question. Asking this kind of question is confusing and distracts students from their ability to respond in a way that assists you in assessing their learning.

H. Ask Your Question before You Call on a Student to Respond

Picture yourself in the following classroom where a teacher could ask a question in either of these two ways. What do you think would be the result in each case?

"Henrietta, how could you improve this sentence?"

"How could you improve this sentence?" (Pause) "Henrietta."

Chances are that in phrasing the first question above, only Henrietta is alerted to concentrate on an answer. In the second question all students are alerted and many are likely to volunteer by raising their hands before the teacher calls on Henrietta.

Always be sure to call on one specific student to respond and make sure that you *call on that student by name*. If you allow students to call out, it will lead to chaos. Also, calling out provides the opportunity for those who do not want to pay attention or participate in class to let others take over.

I. Gear Your Questions to the Ability Levels of the Students

Your goal is to have meaningful participation from *all* students to ensure their success. To accomplish this goal, you have to address the learning needs of diverse students. They differ in readiness, interests, and learning style. For example, big-picture questions could be directed to holistic learners and detail questions to sequential learners. More space and time could be given to introverts who prefer listening and absorbing information and may be better able to answer summarizing questions.

Call on students when you are confident that they will be able to answer correctly by targeting their ability, interest, and readiness level. This *may* mean that at times you will address less demanding questions to some and more demanding questions to others, while expecting high achievement from all. Your ultimate objective should require all to consider essential understandings at high cognitive levels but at varying degrees of difficulty so that all your students are challenged.

J. Distribute Your Questions So That Everyone Has a Chance to Participate

You will want all students to feel as though they are part of your instruction and that their input is important. Keep your antennae out so that you are aware of who has and who has not had the opportunity to respond, and call on everyone at least once. Frequently scan the room to determine not only who has not responded but also who may be confused, irritated, or who may lack interest. Remind students that you care about their participation because *the more they participate, the more they achieve*.

Be aware of the fact that teachers tend to treat boys and girls differently in schools. Much of what is known about this treatment comes from the work of Sadker and Sadker (1994, 1997) and from a report of the American Association of University Women (1992). You should be familiar with the results of the research so that you will implement instruction in your class in which boys and girls have equal expectations and opportunities for success.

The research cited above has reported that girls are more frequently underchallenged and that both male and female teachers in general tended to treat boys and girls differently. According to Sadker and Sadker (1994), during questioning boys are

encouraged more than girls,
called on more often,
asked more higher-level questions,
given more reinforcement for their responses, whether correct or not, and
probed more often for their responses.

On the other side of the coin, it should be noted that other studies found that boys are subject to greater inequities than girls in schools (Sommers, 1996) and that in some situations girls are given preferential treatment and in other situations boys are given preferences (Lee, Chen, & Smerdon, 1996).

As far as you are concerned, it is your responsibility to be cognizant of the tendency for treating boys and girls inequitably in different situations, and to ensure that during your questioning as well as in all other instructional activities, you avoid any gender bias in your own classroom.

To elicit full participation, in some situations it would be beneficial to have students answer in full sentences or to write their responses to questions. When answering in a full sentence, the students must listen to the question, process it, and then integrate the question and answer into a complete thought.

This integration may help improve composition writing skills. For some students, writing answers instead of responding orally could provide a better opportunity for participation. This process could be especially productive for English-language learners, who should be expected to participate, though they may need more time and support to answer the original question and subsequent assistance with the response.

K. Call on Both Volunteers and Nonvolunteers

To avoid the possibility that a few students will dominate the discussion, leaving the rest of the class frustrated (or relieved), call on both volunteers and nonvolunteers. Calling on volunteers encourages them to keep participating. Calling on the nonvolunteers tells them that they are expected to participate. When students do not know when they will be called on, there is an increase in their attention to your questions and to classmates' responses.

However, calling on nonvolunteers must be conducted in a nonthreatening way. Improper teacher body language or verbal tone that communicates impatience or annoyance can turn nonvolunteers off and further discourage them from volunteering or actually responding.

L. Personalize Questions

Whenever appropriate, use the pronoun *you*. Students feel more connected and are more motivated when you ask questions such as, "If *you* were in this situation, what would *you* do?" or "Pretend that *you* are Jim. How would *you* react to his brother?"

M. Use a Collaborative Approach

Situations may occur in which everyone's input on a topic or problem would be helpful. It gives everyone a feeling that she or he is part of a solution. These situations could be managerial or academic. Some examples include:

"How could *we* line up so that everyone can be dismissed safely and quickly?"
"How can *we* solve this triangle problem?"
"How can *we* help each other eat a healthier diet?"

SUMMARY OF EFFECTIVE PRACTICES OF TEACHER PHRASES AND DELIVERY OF QUESTIONS

Secure students' attention before asking a question.

Minimize the number of lower-level questions.

Phrase questions clearly.

Ask questions sequentially.

Use appropriate speed and vocabulary in speaking.

Pause at least 3–5 seconds between asking a question and calling for a response.

Ask one question at a time.

Ask questions before calling on a student.

Personalize questions.

Differentiate questions to students' readiness, learning style, or ability level.

Distribute questions so that all will have the opportunity to respond.

Call on both volunteers and nonvolunteers.

SELF-REFLECTION

- Which practices suggested in this chapter do you implement consistently? Which do you not?
- Are there any suggestions with which you disagree? If so, what is the research base for your disagreement?

④

INEFFECTIVE QUESTIONING PRACTICES WHEN FRAMING AND DELIVERING QUESTIONS

From your own experience and from chapter 3, you should be aware of how complex the effective phrasing and delivery of questions can actually be. Skill in achieving both can significantly increase student participation and achievement. To ensure that this process is as smooth and productive as possible, you should avoid several ineffective framing and delivery questioning behaviors.

A. REPEATING OR REPHRASING QUESTIONS IMMEDIATELY AFTER ASKING THEM

If you have carefully thought through the pivotal questions for the lesson and have secured the students' attention before asking questions, there should be no need to repeat or rephrase them. Yet repeating questions is a common teacher behavior. Repeating questions wastes time. Moreover, if the students know that you will repeat the question, they will tend not to listen the first time.

B. ASKING AND ANSWERING YOUR OWN QUESTIONS

When teachers do not get an immediate response, they sometimes find themselves answering their own questions. This practice defeats the purpose of asking the question in the first place.

You may want to determine why the students may not be responding. Is the question vague? Is it confusing? Do the students have the informational or experiential readiness to answer the question? Assuming that the students have the background to answer the question and that you have framed it properly, you can avoid answering the question yourself by approaching the content from a different perspective by asking a series of developmental questions that will help the students respond or by asking the students why they are having difficulty responding.

For example, if the original question is "Why did the framers of our Constitution want to include a Bill of Rights?" and there is no response from students, it is an effective practice to ask a series of questions that would help elicit a response instead of answering the question yourself:

"What experiences did they (the framers) have in England that would want them to include a Bill of Rights?"

"What freedoms do we have?"

"How do the freedoms in our country allow us to live a fuller life?"

"Think of some countries where there are dictatorships. How would you contrast their way of life with ours?"

"What would life be like if these freedoms were suddenly taken away from us?"

"Why would our framers want to include a Bill of Rights?"

C. ASKING QUESTIONS THAT REQUIRE A CHORUS RESPONSE

When students are asked to respond all together, it leads to calling out and to rewarding those who do not wish to participate. Allowing calling out provides a fertile environment for a few to dominate the class and for an unruly atmosphere that can lead to behavior problems.

However, when students are unsure of a generalization or rule, it would be acceptable to reinforce the content through a chorus response once basic information is understood.

Classroom Clip: Ms. Johnson has listed the following *ei* and *ie* words on the board in two columns. The *ei* or *ie* in each word is underlined and written in colored chalk.

ei words	*ie* words
rec<u>ei</u>ve	retr<u>ie</u>ve
conc<u>ei</u>ve	bel<u>ie</u>ve
perc<u>ei</u>ve	br<u>ie</u>f

Ms. Johnson asks the class if they see any pattern in the *ei* words listed in the first column that is different from the *ie* words. The students should be able to see that the letter "c" precedes the *ei* words.

After they observe this, Ms. Johnson states the rule: "*I* before *e* except after *c*." Ms. Johnson then asks the class to repeat the rule in unison several times. While they state the rule, she points to the *ei* then *c*, demonstrating or having a student demonstrate what the class is stating.

D. ASKING QUESTIONS REQUIRING YES-NO ANSWERS

Questions requiring yes-no answers give students a 50–50 chance of getting the correct answer. Therefore, the answer does not necessarily give the teacher insights regarding students' knowledge. Questions that lead to yes-no responses are not higher-level questions and require only factual information. Examples:

"Did Captain Fred have enough time to dock the boat?"
"Was Kyle happy about her mother's upcoming marriage?"

Another type of yes-no question is "Does everybody understand?" This question is, unfortunately, asked too frequently. What teachers really tell their students when asking this question is that this is their last chance, so that if they don't ask any questions, then this means that the students understand completely, freeing the teacher to move on. The problem is that "sometimes students do not understand that they do not understand, and if they do not know what they do not know, there is no way that they can ask a question about it" (Johnson, 2008).

E. ASKING QUESTIONS REQUIRING ONE-WORD ANSWERS

As in the case of questions requiring yes-no answers, questions requiring one-word responses elicit only factual information and do not develop the cognitive abilities of students. Though these questions may serve some function in a discussion, such as ensuring foundational information or transitioning from one topic to the next, they should be held to a minimum. Read again Mr. Quinn's questions in chapter 3. You will note that five out of his six questions require one-word answers.

F. ASKING LEADING QUESTIONS

Leading questions are the types that restrict students' thinking by limiting their responses and therefore do not provide the teacher with accurate feedback regarding student achievement.

There are three types of leading questions:

- Rhetorical questions
- Questions that contain part of the answer in the question
- Questions that assume the answer in the question

Rhetorical Questions

Rhetorical questions are not questions per se but are statements posed as questions. In effect, these questions are not actually expected to be answered. Rhetorical questions are often intended to have the students agree with the teacher, usually soliciting a "yes" response. If the students do not literally say yes, they will think it. (Once they agree, they will likely also agree with what follows.) Examples:

"Wasn't that a great movie?"
"Didn't that election give great results?"
"Didn't the team do a fabulous job?"

Rhetorical questions are also sometimes used when a teacher hedges, wanting to make a statement but not confident enough to assert a point. Example:

"Wasn't that a great performance? I can't imagine anything better?"

Questions That Contain Part of the Answer

Questions that contain part of the answer in the question or supply part of the answer to complete the question are ineffective in determining student knowledge.

Suppose someone said to you, "Leonardo di _____." You would probably say Caprio (or if you heard da instead of di, you might say Vinci). You have already provided a response, but has anyone asked you a question? Sometimes teachers phrase questions in a way that includes part of the answer. "The hero in the movie *Titanic* is Leonardo di..." Whether or not the student knows the correct answer or not, he or she is able to supply an answer.

Questions That Assume the Answer

Other types of leading questions propose that something is true by hiding it in a question. These questions are structured to guide a person to think in a certain way.

One type solicits agreement, forcing a yes or no response. "Don't you agree that this is an appropriate book for teenagers?" is the type of leading question that implies a student should agree. It would be more effective to say, "Explain why you think that this is or is not an appropriate book for teenagers."

"Isn't that all right?" is another example. This question does not allow for students to respond if they think that something is *not* all right.

Assumptive Questions

Another type of leading question is an *assumptive* question, one that acts that something is true, then hides it in a question. Examples:

"How will you convince them?" (Assumes you will try to convince them)
"When will you change the data?" (Assumes you will change the data)
"Where will you buy your car?" (Assumes you will buy a car)

Linked Statements

You can also lead questions by linked statements. These questions associate a question or statement you use initially, followed by a linked question or statement. Examples:

"Would you prefer to live in San Diego or in Woodbridge, where the crime rate is lower?"
"What is your opinion of Senator _____? So many people are opposed to him, I thought you'd want to know."
"I hate going to this restaurant. What do you think about this place?"

Coercive Questions

Coercive leading questions force specific responses. The coercion can be implicit or explicit. Examples:

"Aren't you coming to the party tonight? There won't be any fun if you're not there."
"How can you not volunteer to set up for the party?"

Tag Questions

Tag questions are short leading questions connected to the end of a statement. They force agreement or compliance by making a command appear as if it were a question by including a negative component. Examples:

"That's a great contribution on her part, isn't it?"
"You'll come to his birthday dinner, won't you?
"You're volunteering to set up for the party, aren't you?"

To summarize, leading questions force students to agree with the question and do not foster them to think independently. "Why did he make the correct decision?" is not the type of question that leaves room for students to disagree with the decision. Better worded, the question would read "What conditions would have made you come to this decision or to a different one?"

Additional examples of leading questions are:

"Why *should* Congress have passed that bill?"
"Explain why the Senate's ideas were *better* than the House's."
"What made this story *great*?"
"Why was this the *best* plan?"
"What did you *like* about the poem?"

Go back and identify the assumptions in the above five questions, then rephrase them so that they can unleash more thoughtful responses from students.

G. UNPROFESSIONAL PHRASING

Teachers should avoid phrasing questions as direct statements that end up as questions:

"The function of the gall bladder is what?"
"The gall bladder is located where?"

These "questions" should be phrased

"What is the function of the gall bladder?"
"Where is the gall bladder located?

Clumsy wording also occurs when the teacher asks questions that end in prepositions. Note how much smoother the phrasing of the second question is in the following two examples:

"Which flask should this solution be poured into?"
"Into which flask should we pour this solution?"

Other unprofessionally worded questions are: "Who knows . . .?" "Who can tell the class . . . ?" or "Does anyone know . . . ?" It is more effective to ask the question, pause, and then call on a student to respond.

Along with unprofessional phrasing of questions are comments such as "Okay?" or "All right?" introduced after statements or directions. These comments make the teacher seem insecure. Examples:

"We will finish the last three paragraphs, okay?"
"Stay on the right side as we walk down the hall, all right?"

SUMMARY OF INEFFECTIVE PRACTICES OF TEACHER PHRASES AND DELIVERY OF QUESTIONS

Immediately repeating or rephrasing questions after asking them
Asking and answering your own questions
Asking questions that elicit a chorus response
Asking questions that elicit a yes-no response
Asking questions that call for one-word answers
Asking leading questions
Phrasing questions unprofessionally

SELF-REFLECTION

- Are you aware of any ineffective questioning practices that you implement in your classroom? Have you audio/video recorded your teaching to identify any ineffective questioning behaviors?
- Are there ineffective questioning practices offered in this chapter with which you disagree? If so, what is the research base for your disagreement?

(5)

EFFECTIVE QUESTIONING PRACTICES WHEN RESPONDING TO STUDENTS' ANSWERS

You will recall that in Phase 1 the teacher poses and delivers a question. The student then provides a response in Phase 2.

HOW STUDENTS MAY RESPOND

Students may respond in any of the following ways:

Provide no response
Refuse to answer
State they do not know
Give the correct response
Offer a partially correct response
Provide an incorrect response
State they did not hear the question
Offer an unexpected response
Answer in a silly way
Call out

Can you think of other ways students may respond?

During the time that a student responds (or does not respond), you must be a careful listener and observer. You need to also be aware of the reasons that some students may be hesitant to respond to your question. Among these reasons are your expectation of an immediate response, not knowing the answer or having difficulty expressing it, not being sure of the question as expressed, anxiety regarding failure or ridicule, apathy, and a general fear of expressing responses publicly. All of these will be diminished if you have already taken the time to structure a positive and supportive classroom environment.

If a student does choose to respond, the content may be influenced by his or her past experience with success or failure; age; culture; past experience with similar situations involved in the question; peer beliefs; personal values, biases, and beliefs; or prior learning (Chuska, 1995).

Occasionally, a student may respond by asking a question. If this should occur, ask the class how *they* would answer the question instead of immediately answering it yourself.

At this point, it must be emphasized that you should train students to answer in a tone that can be *heard* by the entire class. Reticent students and those who are unsure will tend to speak more softly and perhaps even inaudibly. Yet these students should understand that their input is important and that everyone wants to share in that input, regardless of what the student presently knows, because the goal of a supportive class is to have everyone feel comfortable and achieve.

It ought to be noted that you should not interrupt a student who is trying to respond, especially when that student is making a sincere effort. This student needs time and patience from the entire classroom community.

EFFECTIVE RESPONSES TO STUDENTS' ANSWERS

There is much spontaneity that occurs in classrooms, and there are no set formulas that teachers can follow to react to students' responses. Questioning is not only a skill but also an art. Most questioning and responding requires that teachers think on their feet. However, there are some techniques teachers can use to keep their talking to a minimum while keeping students involved and promoting higher-level thinking.

Here, the quality of teacher feedback determines how student knowledge will be enhanced.

Positive (effective) questioning in Phase 3 includes several practices.

A. Increasing Wait-Time 2

Frequently, teachers are so quick to respond to a student's answer—waiting less than 1 second—that they do not give themselves enough time to consider the answer, to come up with a cogent reaction, to provide enough time for the responding student to complete his or her thought, for other students to respond to the same question, or for students to react to each other's answers. You have already read about wait-time 1, the time between the teacher asking a question and calling on a student to respond. Wait-time 2 is the time between a student's answer and the teacher's resumption of speaking.

Increasing wait-time 2 to at least 3 seconds before providing feedback, cuing, probing, or redirecting has been positively correlated with student achievement (White & Tisher, 1986). Here again, as in wait-time 1, if you have not been taking the time to respond to students' answers, inform the class that you will be taking this time and the reasons for it.

B. Give Some Feedback to a Student's Answer

It is generally agreed that some feedback should be given to a student's answer. "Feedback provides immediacy and impact to an activity" (Good & Brophy, 1997, p. 229). No feedback given to a student's response, *even if the answer is correct*, is often perceived as negative feedback. You should also note that students would rather know their answer was incorrect (receive negative feedback) than have no knowledge of results at all.

Brophy (1979) concluded that the attributes of effective feedback are:

- *Honesty*. If you praise a student for an incorrect response, your praise will eventually be ignored by all students. Accepting an incorrect response just to make a student feel good does not extend his or her ability to achieve.
- *Contingency*. Answers that are correct should be praised; answers that are incorrect should be corrected.

- *Specificity*. Students should know exactly what deserves praise ("You answered that question on a very mature level.") and what needs correction ("Check the irregular verb list I distributed for past participles.")

Teacher praise for a student's answer can be given *when warranted* by changing the mode of response so that it does not become boring and ineffectual. "Good," "Great," "Super," "Good thinking," "Great insight," "Fine job," "Never thought of that myself," "You really worked hard," and equivalent statements are just a few of the responses you can give students. Other statements of praise such as "Wow" or "Wonderful" are frequently listed on posters displayed throughout many schools.

It should be pointed out that some educators believe that praise can be problematic (Kohn, 2001; Tauber, 2007). They see praise as manipulative, something teachers do to force students to cooperate. Praise may increase students' dependence on the teacher instead of having students participating for their own sake. Dreikurs (1998) promotes the practice of praising effort rather than performance because effort is within the student's control whereas innate ability that could lead to higher performance levels is not.

Recent research has concluded that praise is linked to the difference in perception in how students view their intelligence: between those who view their intelligence as fixed and those who believe that intelligence can be improved through effort.

Praise for intelligence tends to lead students to a fixed mind-set resulting in a lack of motivation and resilience; praise for effort is more conducive to developing a growth mind-set, which fosters working hard (Dweck, 2008). She recommends "process" praise (feedback) for involvement, perseverance, and growth, which all nurture robust motivation. Process praise informs students what they have done in order to achieve success and what they can do to repeat that success. Examples of process praise that teachers can use in response to what effort students have made to answer questions include:

"Wow! You really thought through that answer. It showed how you were able to go back and put together what you already knew. Congratulations."

"That was a tough question, but you stayed with it until you integrated so many different ideas. Kudos."

"Putting that answer together took a lot of thinking. It showed how your effort led us all see the situation much clearer. Thanks."

In Phase 3 (the teacher responds to the student's answer), the most appropriate teacher feedback comes in reaction to *specific* responses of students.

C. If a Student Did Not Hear the Question, Ask Another Student to Repeat It

Classroom Clip:

Teacher: What are some major problems that must be confronted when considering health-care reform? (Pause) Judy.

Judy: What was the question again?

Teacher: Please tell Judy what I just asked. (Pause) Pete.

This teacher response conveys a subliminal message that the student called on should have been listening in the first place. Of course, this teacher response assumes that she or he had everyone's attention before asking the question.

D. Encourage Sustained Responses from Students

It has been reported that encouraging student responses so that they express their own ideas, personal opinions, experiences, and understandings makes the class more student centered. Correspondingly, students' answers are longer, more articulate, and reflect a higher level of thinking (Oliveira, 2010).

This effect is evidenced not only with students but also with teachers. It was confirmed that even teacher educators needed to elicit, reframe, or clarify teachers' ideas, press for elaboration, check for interpretation, and connect the content presented with their classroom experiences when providing professional development (Zhang et al., 2010).

These types of sustained responses can be encouraged in several ways. If the student's answer is *correct*, ask for further clarification or probe by asking a few follow-up questions that develop answers more fully. Probing can provide new insights for students or take what they already know to higher levels.

The following example is an adaptation of probing and asking for further clarification offered by Sadker & Sadker (1999, p. 131).

Teacher: How can we convince auto manufacturers to build smaller cars, cars that burn less gasoline?

Student: Pass a law.

Teacher: Can you be more specific? (*asking for further clarification*)

Student: Sure. Put a limit on the size of cars.

Teacher: Why do you think that would work? (*probing*)

Student: Well, smaller cars burn less gas. If you just ask them to make smaller cars, they wouldn't do it. So pass a law requiring it.

Teacher: How do you think car manufacturers would react to being forced to make smaller cars? (*probing*)

Student: They probably wouldn't like it, but they would do it.

Teacher: What effect might such a law have on businesspeople in other industries? (*probing*)

In this example, the teacher has asked for further clarification and probed the student's answer. The result led to the development of insights involved in simply passing a law to solve a problem. Other examples of probing questions are:

"What additional information do you need to solve that problem?"
"What would you have to do to get that information?"

Using Funnel Questions to Probe

When responding to your questions, students may offer information that is too general or too detailed. You can probe either type of response by funnel questioning. If you are looking for more detail, you can narrow the funnel. This process is similar to that used in deductive reasoning in which the thinking proceeds from general to specific. "Tell me more about . . ." is a general question that guides the responder to give you more information. Since it is an open question, it permits the responder more leeway and gets more detail, even though it may take more time.

Classroom Clip:

Student: We want to go on vacation.

Teacher: Tell me more about that.

Student: We went away last year and want to go again this year?

Teacher: Where did you go last year?

Student: Florida.

Teacher: What part?

Student: Key West.

Teacher: What did you do there?

Student: Snorkel.

Teacher: Anything else?

Student: We rode on dolphins.

Teacher: Would you like to do this again or something different?

Student: Probably a little bit of that and something new.

Teacher: What would be included in something new?

Student: Mountain climbing.

Teacher: Wow, that's quite different from snorkeling. Which would you prefer?

Student: Can't tell.

Teacher: If you were forced to choose, which type of vacation would you take?

Student: (A long pause). Well, we had such a blast last year, I would probably prefer going snorkeling again. (Another long pause) Then next year we could plan on mountain climbing.

Questions that employ words such as "specifically," "actually," or "particularly" will also frequently gain more detail from students. Examples:

> "What *specifically* did June say that made you know she was planning to leave?"
> "When *exactly* did you decide to make your career choice?"
> "Who *in particular* seemed to gain most by her uncle's death?"

If a student responds to your question with specific information, you may want to probe him by asking questions that elicit information about more general topics. Decreasing the amount of detail is analogous to inductive reasoning in which thinking proceeds from specific to more general.

You can widen the funnel by focusing questions that provide less detail about a small area and increase information about related topics. "What other things," "Who else," "What else" can help obtain this kind of information. Examples:

> "Who else can be included in the club?"
> "What other activities could the club provide?"

Follow-Up Questions

If the student says she doesn't know the answer or provides a weak or incorrect answer, you can provide cueing for that student to offer some follow-up questions that will lead her to a correct response.

Classroom Clip:

Teacher: What is an adjective?

Student: I'm not sure.

Teacher: Last week we played a concept attainment game where you were supposed to learn about adjectives. What were some of the words in our Example column?

Student: Uh, uh . . . blue, uh, oh yeah, pretty, fat.

Teacher: Give me a sentence with the word blue.

Student: John is wearing a blue shirt.

Teacher: What does blue tell you about the shirt?

Student: Tells what it looks like.

Teacher: What's another word for telling what something looks like.

Student: Describes.

Teacher: What word is blue describing?

Student: Shirt.

Teacher: What part of speech is shirt?

Student: Uh, a noun.

Teacher: So what is an adjective?

Student: Oh yeah, I remember now. A word that describes a noun.

Teacher: Good thinking.

Redirecting

If a student does not respond, you can cue him, or say you will get back to him, then use *redirecting* in which you ask the same question (without repeating it) to one or several other students. When the answer or deepened perspective regarding the answer is finally elicited, go back to the original student and have him repeat the answer or put it in his own words. The point is to have the original student learn and receive satisfaction that he has responded correctly. And besides, when the student verbalizes a correct answer, it reinforces and thereby helps retain that answer.

Classroom Clip:

Teacher: We've been studying mammals for several days. What are some of the characteristics of mammals? (Pause) Henry.

Henry: (No response)

Teacher: Martin?

Martin: They have hair or fur.

Teacher: Excellent, why would they need hair or fur?

Martin: They're warm-blooded.

Teacher: True. Can anyone think of anything else that makes mammals different? (Pause) Robert.

Robert: They breast-feed their young.

Teacher: That's right. And one way to remember that is to think of the connection between mammals and mammary glands. Now, Henry (*goes back to first student to whom she asked the question*), can you tell us some characteristics of mammals?

Henry: They have hair or fur and mammary glands to feed their babies.

Teacher: Great, Henry. I knew you knew it.

An interesting analysis of a student's incorrect answer was made by Robin Hunter (2004). He pointed out that when a student provides an incorrect answer, there are two things she does not know: the correct answer to the question, and the question to which the incorrect answer belongs. Hunter offers as an example that when a student is asked how much 5×7 is and responds that it is 30, she does not know that $5 \times 7 = 35$ and that $5 \times 6 = 30$. As a result. there are *two* facts the student must learn. He proposes teaching *both* by using the following procedures:

1. *Dignify the student's response by supplying the question or statement to which the answer belongs.* "You would be right if I asked 5×6 because 5×6 equals 30. You are in the five times table." Your comment tells the student, "You had something important to offer; you simply got it in the wrong place.
2. *Then, give the student an assist or prompt,* since our function as teachers is to help students be right, not to catch them being wrong. "Suppose I ask you to buy six packages of gum for a nickel each. If you bought one more package for yourself, at a nickel per package, seven packages of gum would cost how much?" (You could also draw this on the board and have the student add the number of fives six times to get 30. Then add to the drawing one more piece of gum and have the student add the extra nickel to the 30 to get 35.)
3. *Finally, hold that student accountable.* It's important to assist the student, but it is equally important to insist that the student learn and remember. [With the drawing still on the board, go back and ask how much 5×7 is, and then what number multiplied by 5 equals 30]. . . .

"I'll bet you'll remember that if I ask you the same question tomorrow." The unmistakable message is "I expect you to." (Hunter 2004, p. 111; bracketed additions mine)

At this point in the discussion of questioning, it is important to remind you that students from different cultures and students with exceptionalities may view teacher questioning and reactions to responses differently. To ensure equity in dealing with all students, remember that:

- With Asian Americans, where shyness is valued, a student *may* not volunteer and avoid eye contact so that he or she will not be called on.
- Students whose native language is not English *may* need a wait time longer than 3–5 seconds to respond.
- Hispanic females, when in a class with males, *may* be observers during the discussion in the classroom rather than demonstrate academic prowess.
- Native Americans *may* be ill-at-ease when cued or probed.
- Teachers *may* ask more questions of boys than girls, direct more questions involving higher levels of thinking to boys, and provide them with longer wait time.
- Learning-disabled (LD) students *may* have difficulty answering questions at higher levels. LD students need more time to practice higher-level responses and more time to process questions. It is sometimes helpful for students with learning disabilities to write answers to questions.

Observe that the word "may" was used in all the above examples to avoid stereotyping. It is difficult and often frustrating for teachers who want to be equitable to deal with the diversity in their classrooms. The best way to handle the diversity in your class is to *explain ahead of time* what you will do and *why* you are doing it. For example, tell the students that you will call on both volunteers and nonvolunteers. Then explain that the reason you will do this is that you want everyone to achieve and it has been proven that the more they participate, the more they achieve.

It should also be noted that in considering multiple intelligences, the questioning interaction described in this chapter favors students with linguistic intelligence. Howard Gardner (1995) has expressed his concern that the emphasis in school is on linguistic and mathematical-logical intelligences. You might consider expanding the verbal responses of students to questions that can be expressed in different intelligences. Examples:

"Which of your personal assets can you draw on to solve this problem?"
"Can you act out the way you feel?"
"With whom could you work to construct your questions?"
"Can you make a drawing of your idea?"

SUMMARY OF EFFECTIVE PRACTICES OF TEACHER RESPONSES TO A STUDENT'S ANSWER

Increase wait-time 2.
Give some feedback to a student's answer.
Ask a student to repeat the question for a student who did not hear it.
Encourage sustained responses through redirecting, probing, cuing, and funneling.
Be sensitive to cultural differences and exceptionalities in student responses.

SELF-REFLECTION

- Which practices suggested in this chapter do you implement consistently? Which do you not?
- Are there any suggestions with which you disagree? If so, what is the research base for your disagreement?

(6)

INEFFECTIVE QUESTIONING PRACTICES WHEN RESPONDING TO STUDENTS' ANSWERS

In their anxiety to get answers from students, teachers will often engage in behavior that actually impedes the learning process and discourages students from participating. Some of these inappropriate questioning behaviors include the following tendencies.

A. REPEATING THE STUDENT'S ANSWER (RESPONSE)

If you observe classroom questioning, you may be surprised that it is common for teachers to immediately repeat students' answers. This practice seems difficult for teachers to avoid just as is the practice of increasing the wait time after asking a question. Some teachers may think that they are rewarding students by repeating their answers, reinforcing correct answers, or repeating students' answers so that they can be heard by all class members.

You should train your students to answer in a tone that everyone can hear so that repeating answers is not necessary. In a contemporary classroom that fosters student support and cooperation, you want to ensure that students listen to each other.

If you emphasize that you value what all students have to say and that it is all right to make a mistake, and if you conduct your questioning sessions in a nonthreatening way, students will feel more confident speaking up. Besides, repeating students' answers becomes boring and it subtly signals the rest of the class that they do not have to listen to each other.

B. TUGGING QUESTIONS

When the teacher has elicited enough information but tries to pull (tug) more information, the additional information becomes meaningless. Example:

In a classroom where five attributes of Impressionist paintings are already listed on the board, the teacher says, "Who can give me just one more attribute of these paintings?" The students take a deep breath, then groan with frustration. Be aware of when you have elicited enough information from students, then move on.

C. REACTING IN A DISCOURAGING OR DISAPPOINTING MANNER TO ANSWERS

As a teacher, you already know to expect the unexpected. Teachers, especially novices, tend to frame questions that have pat answers. As teachers expand their repertoires to include more divergent questions, students may not answer the way teachers have anticipated, causing them to sometimes react in a negative and discouraging way.

Borich (2007) provides an example of an inappropriate reaction to un-expected answers. When you read the script, stop after the first teacher reaction to Student 1 and think of what response you might expect from the student before reading the rest of the interchange.

Teacher: OK, today we will study the European settlers who came to America and why they came here. Why did they come to America?

Student 1: To farm.

Teacher: No, not to farm.

Student 2: To build houses and churches.

Teacher: No, that's not right either (Borich, 2007, p. 326).

How would you feel if you were Student 1 or Student 2? How could you use effective questioning practices already described in this book to build on an incorrect answer to get the appropriate student response?

A teacher could ask Student 1 for further clarification by saying, "While farming was of interest to some people, there were more important reasons Europeans wanted to come here. Can you think of any others?"

A teacher could probe Student 2 by asking, "Why would churches be important?" This question would eventually lead to the fact that some Europeans came here for religious liberty.

The teacher should try to accept the students' answers, even if incorrect, in a positive way and try to build on the responses to lead the student to the correct answer.

D. PARAPHRASING

Paraphrasing a student's response in a way that actually corrects an incorrect answer offered by the student is another ineffective technique. Example:

Teacher: Why did Europeans come to America?

Student: To farm

Teacher: While some were interested in farming, others came for religious liberty.

E. INAPPROPRIATE BODY LANGUAGE

Several studies (Brophy, 1979; Siegman & Feldstein, 1987) have suggested that nonverbal communication (body language) is perceived as *more powerful* than verbal communication by most students. Frowning, scowling, head shaking, hands on hips, eye rolling, foot tapping, or taking a deep breath and exhaling with a loud puff can discourage students from participating.

Also, pointing at a student either by using the whole hand or a finger instead of calling that student by name when eliciting a response is viewed as accusatory and impersonal—yet pointing at students when calling on them is a common practice of many teachers.

SUMMARY OF *INEFFECTIVE* PRACTICES OF TEACHER RESPONSES TO A STUDENT'S ANSWER

Repeating a student's answer

Soliciting too much information (overkill)

Reacting in a discouraging way to unexpected answers

Paraphrasing a student's answer in a way that actually answers an incorrect answer

Inappropriate body language

SELF-REFLECTION

- Are you aware of any practices suggested in this chapter that you implement consistently? That you do not? Have you ever confirmed your perceptions through audio/video recording your classes?
- Are there any suggestions with which you disagree? If so, what is the research base for your disagreement?

⑦

ENCOURAGING
STUDENT QUESTIONING

In a contemporary classroom that encourages students to write questions for tests, assist in writing criteria for rubrics, and monitor their own progress in achieving behavioral and cognitive goals, students should also be encouraged to ask questions about academic content. Yet one of the most neglected questioning skills of teachers has been eliciting these types of questions from students (Walsh & Sattes, 2005).

Focusing on student questioning and valuing these questions as opposed to emphasizing responses is critical for teachers who want to move from a teacher-centered to a student-centered classroom (Albergaria-Almeida, 2010). Moreover, it has been reported that students enjoyed reading each other's questions and became more interested in deeper understanding (Drozynski et al., 2010).

When students are first asked to formulate questions, it is an eye-opener for teachers because the students frequently mirror teachers' behavior. Just as teachers must learn and practice effective questioning skills, so must students. They can be assisted in developing questioning skills in several ways:

GENERAL WAYS TO ENCOURAGE QUESTIONS FROM STUDENTS

Ensure that you have established a warm and caring classroom environment for your students. This open environment will result in a positive emotional climate that is personal and is risk free. Students who feel personally connected with their teachers and with their classmates ask a higher number of questions (Newman & Schwager, 1993).

To further accentuate the importance of establishing a positive emotional environment, recent research by Cayanus (2011) identified the main reasons why students do *not* ask questions. These include fear, class size (the larger the class, the less some students participate), not wanting to talk (which is more pervasive in a large class), and the teacher's attitude and skill.

Show that students' questions are valued. Sometimes students will ask irrelevant questions during a lesson, and the teacher, desiring to stay on task, will tell the students that the question has nothing to do with the lesson. However, if the teacher reserves a space on the board or displays a poster with a title equivalent to "Questions We Want to Explore" where questions can be recorded during the lesson and pursued later, the teacher can then immediately go back to the lesson, and the students will be rewarded for their questions. It is important that there then be *follow-through* on exploring recorded questions.

Have the students make a habit of writing questions at the end of a lesson; at the end of a chapter or unit; before and after a field trip, video, or visit by a resource person; and during their reading. Research has shown that when students are required to generate questions about material they have studied or have read, there is a significant improvement in comprehension (King & Rosenshine, 1993).

Write the lesson objective on the board in the form of a question. When the lesson is completed, go back to that question, have the students answer it, then ask for additional questions. Example:

Write the question, "How can we compute the area of a circle?" instead of the objective, "To compute the area of a circle." Ask the students to answer the question and then ask them if they have any other questions.

Encourage the formulation and phrasing of students' questions by *modeling* these questions.

For example, when discussing what students have read, ask questions such as

"What is the point the author is trying to make?"
"What does the author assume? Imply?"
"From what point of view or frame of reference is the author coming?"
"What may be the author's biases?"
"What main questions or problems does the author pose?"
"What evidence does the author provide to support his position?"
"What are the author's conclusions?"
"Does the evidence the author offered justify the conclusions?"

Types of questions that model higher-level thinking in students in any subject could also include:

"What is the main point . . . ?"
"How is this related to . . . ?"
"What are the positives and negatives of . . . ?"
"How is . . . different or the same?"
"What can you conclude from . . . ?"

In addition, unexpectedly thoughtful discussions can be provoked by "What would happen if . . . ? (Drozynski et al., 2010).

Most important, if the teacher does not know the answer to a question, she should display a "let's find out" attitude where the teacher and the students can pursue the answer together, and from that answer generate more questions.

Invite students to question each other using the same positive practices suggested in Phases 1 and 3. Reinforce what you should already have established in creating a positive classroom atmosphere: that during the questioning, students must be courteous to each other, not monopolize the discussion, address each other by name, and consider each question carefully before framing it.

Use authentic questions. Students are more motivated to ask further questions when stimulated by *personally relevant* questions and those that arouse their interest in accordance with their age and stage of development.

Teach students how to question. Questioning is a skill that can be learned, and students should learn the same skills addressed in this book. Depending on the maturity of students, teach them the difference between open and closed questions, the need for pausing, and even how to improve their questioning levels according to different taxonomies (chapter 8).

Take a few moments to share with your students what *you* learned as a result of their responses to questions and to questions they have asked you and the class. This action communicates to students more effectively the value you place on their participations and their questions.

SPECIFIC WAYS TO ENCOURAGE QUESTIONS FROM STUDENTS

Brainstorming

Although originally developed as a technique for creative problem-solving, brainstorming can also be used as a method for student questioning. Brainstorming is particularly effective because it reduces fear of failure and fosters the opportunity for all students to participate without being judged.

After an appropriate amount of instruction, students gather in groups to brainstorm as many questions as they can about the content to which they were already exposed and other questions they may want to pursue. A recorder lists all questions, which are eventually placed into categories. Students can explore the questions individually, as a group, or with the teacher.

Reverse Questioning

Provide students with an answer, and then request that they formulate questions that would lead to that answer. For example, if you give the students the answer 10, some questions among an infinite number that the students might ask could be:

"What is 10 divided by 1?"
"What is 10 plus or minus 0?"
"What is the largest number, other than 20 itself, that is a factor of 20?"
"What number is 10 raised to the first power?"

Use the Inquiry Training Strategy

Suchman (1962) used this strategy for teaching science by introducing a discrepant event that the students would have to reconcile through questions that could only be formulated to elicit a yes or no response. His strategy can also be used with a puzzle or riddle.

To implement the inquiry strategy:

Introduce a riddle or another discrepant event.
Have the students ask questions posed in such a way that they *can be answered only by yes or no.*
Allow no opinion questions, only data-seeking questions.
Allow only one student at a time to have the floor. This student may keep asking questions until he or she runs out of ideas.
Occasionally have the students call a conference to summarize and discuss what they learned from the yes-no responses before continuing the questioning.

This strategy allows the student to do the thinking, the questioning, and most of the talking.

A popular riddle commonly used to illustrate this strategy is: "A man is afraid to go home because of the man with the mask. Why?"

The students may begin to solve the riddle by framing questions that can only be answered yes or no. They can continue by following the rest of the steps described above. (One possible answer to the riddle is at the end of the chapter.)

Reciprocal Teaching

Reciprocal teaching (Palinscar & Brown, 1989) can be used with any age group and content area that requires reading as either instruction or as follow-up after instruction. The teacher first presents to the class no more than four procedures for cultivating and monitoring reading comprehension, for example, predicting, questioning, clarifying, and summarizing. These procedures are then practiced by reading relevant texts and literature.

The teacher models the entire process. Students are placed in groups where they make predictions about what they are to read. After reading a designated part of the material, the teacher asks questions about the content and the group discusses the questions. The group talks its way through the content, a group member summarizes the content, and other group members clarify content.

After at least 20 hours of practice in which the teacher has been the leader, a new group discussion leader assumes the process (predicting, questioning, clarifying, and summarizing) and then the group comes up with a new set of predictions about the next section to be read. As the role of group leader is rotated, more students within the group have the opportunity to ask questions.

When implementing reciprocal teaching, the teacher must make sure that control is transferred to the students *gradually*, that task difficulty and responsibility correspond to each student's ability, and that each student's teaching performance is observed to determine that particular student's thought process and the type of remedial instruction that student may need to be a successful participant (Rosenshine & Meister, 1994; Marzano, 2007).

Reciprocal Questioning

Reciprocal questioning can be used to develop deeper understanding of content. Using this process, students, usually in groups of two or three, ask and then take turns answering questions about a lesson. However, the questions are not those developed independently by the students but are those structured by question stems provided by the teacher. The question stems facilitate the students' ability to connect the new content with previously learned material or experience. Some examples of question stems include (King, 2002, p. 37):

"How is this (situation) the same and different from . . . ?"
"Why do you agree (or disagree) with this conclusion?"

"What evidence can you give to support your conclusion?"
"What is a different example of . . . ?"
"How could you implement . . . in this situation?"
"Explain how . . . affects . . . . What does . . . mean?"
"How is this connected to what we studied before?"
"Why would you conclude that . . . ?"

Questioning the Textbook

Ask the students to go through different paragraphs in the textbook. For every declarative sentence, have the students write a question that the declarative sentence would answer. Then ask other students to answer the question.

You could also ask your students to make up their own strategies or create strategies based on popular programs. For example, students could act as TV hosts like Jay Leno or David Letterman and develop questions that could be asked of guests (other students). Or students can come up with their own games such as "Think Tank." The teacher then poses a problem such as "What can be done about illegal immigration?" Students ask questions about the problem and then research possible solutions.

Answer to riddle presented in the Inquiry Training Strategy. The man with the mask is a baseball catcher stationed at home plate.

SELF-REFLECTION

- Do you encourage your students to ask questions? If so, how?
- Are you satisfied with your students' level of involvement? If not, what will you do to engage them in this process?

(8)

USING TAXONOMIES TO
FORMULATE QUESTIONS

Bloom et al. (1956) were pioneers in getting teachers and students to plan objectives on all levels of the cognitive domain. You can also use their taxonomy as well as the taxonomies of other educators as a framework to assist you in planning questions that will stretch your students to respond at all levels. The taxonomies represent an incremental framework of complex skills that will engage students in demonstrating mastery of content. Research has indicated that memory is enhanced when students are engaged with topics at higher levels (Garavalia et al., 1999).

Even highly experienced teachers have difficulty formulating questions higher than those involving simple memory. Teacher themselves must do higher-level thinking in order to pose such questions. It also takes knowledge of each level, identification of questions at each level, and practice, practice, and more practice.

BLOOM'S TAXONOMY

All authors of subsequent taxonomies have acknowledged in their work the groundbreaking contribution of Bloom et al. (1956). Therefore, Bloom's taxonomy will be presented first.

Level 1: Knowledge

On the knowledge level, the student is asked to remember facts by simply recalling or recognizing information. At this level, students can recall pictures, landmarks, songs, lists, sequences, titles, names, movements, and rituals.

Words commonly associated with the knowledge level include:

define	recite	what
describe	choose	where
identify	state	when
list	recognize	label
name	remember	locate
recall	who	show

Mr. Quinn's questions (chapter 3) are examples of knowledge-level questions. Other examples are:

"What is the capital of Colorado?"
"From where does the United States import most of its coffee?"
"What is a criterion-referenced test?"

You will recall that memory questions are *still important* and often necessary because they involve the only thought process that provides the building blocks for higher information levels. Acquiring broad generalized knowledge is required before moving on to higher levels. Factual questions can also serve as transition questions. It is the *overuse* of memory questions that you should learn to avoid.

Level 2: Comprehension

The comprehension level requires the student to go beyond recalling information by taking that information and demonstrating sufficient understanding of it to make comparisons or to restate or describe it in his or her own words. At this level, the student demonstrates learning of content from a personalized, internalized perspective.

Words commonly associated with the comprehension level are:

compare	describe	relate
contrast	explain	summarize

convert   paraphrase
classify   put in your own words

Examples of comprehension-level questions are:

"How would you describe the giraffe we saw at the zoo?"
"Could you put in your own words the main idea of this paragraph?"
"How would you compare and contrast communism with socialism?"

Level 3: Application

On the application level, the student must use information gathered at the knowledge and comprehension levels and apply or use this information to solve a problem. The student creates new examples from principles learned that relate to a new situation.

Words commonly associated with the application level are:

apply	employ	translate
choose	give an example	use
classify	how many	which
construct	operate	what is
demonstrate	solve	

Examples of application-level questions are:

"Which rules of grammar have been applied in this paragraph?"
"Which examples of punctuation errors can you find in this paragraph?"
"How would you draw a diagonal to bisect this parallelogram?"

As you continue through the levels, think of what prior information and mental processes are needed to perform at each level. Consider, for example, what basic information students would need to answer the question "What are the attributes of the first piano concertos of Mozart and Tchaikovsky that would affect a listener's emotions differently?"

Note that frequently the same word is used to question at different levels. The words that follow the initial word(s) determine the question's level. An illustration is using "What" as the first word of a question. For example, "*What* is the largest city in the United States?" requires a different mental activity level from "*What* would the United States be like now if the Axis had won the war?"

Level 4: Analysis

On the analysis level, the student breaks information down into the sum of its parts and organizes those parts into meaningful new relationships. The student is asked to provide reasons for information by formulating conclusions, providing inferences and generalizations, and most importantly, coming up with reasons for the inferences and generalizations.

Words commonly associated with the analysis level are:

analyze	distinguish between or	relate
arrange	among	support
break down	draw a conclusion	why
determine what evidence	explain	
differentiate	point out	

Examples of questions on the analysis level are:

"What information would you use to support the impeachment of the president?"
"How would you relate the reasons for slavery with the economy of the South?"
"How were the causes of World War I and World War II different?"

Level 5: Synthesis

On the synthesis level, the student is asked to connect knowledge with other knowledge. This information is then used in new ways such as predicting conditions that do not currently exist, coming up with a unique solution to a problem, or creating a new response to a situation.

Words often associated with the synthesis level include:

compare	develop	how would you solve
construct	devise	predict
create	formulate	produce
design	how would you improve	speculate

Examples of synthesis-level questions are:

"How would you redesign the traffic flow so we'd have less congestion?"
"What supporting reasons would you include in a letter to the editor for disagreeing with the editorial?"
"How would our lives be different if we abandoned all rules?"

Level 6: Evaluation

Evaluation means determining whether information or arguments are sound or not. On the evaluation level, a student is asked to form decisions and judgments based on clear, predetermined criteria.

Words commonly associated with the evaluation level include:

appraise	defend	what is your opinion
argue	why do you agree	which solution would be better
assess	evaluate	justify
critique	judge	
decide	prioritize	

Examples of evaluation-level questions are:

"Why would the author of this article believe that Beethoven is a more competent composer than Tchaikovsky?"
"What defense can you give for supporting or not supporting whether multicultural issues should be considered in the classroom?"
"Using the criteria we developed for living standards, how would you decide which country would be ranked the highest?"

The Task-Oriented Question Construction Wheel, figure 8.1, is an example of how both questions and activities can be used to implement Bloom's taxonomy.

THE TAXONOMY OF GALLAGHER AND ASCHER

Gallagher and Ascher (1963) have also offered a taxonomy that can be used for questioning. As with all taxonomies, theirs is a hierarchical

Table 8.1. Bloom's Cognitive Domain

Levels	Task	Corresponding Verbs
Knowledge	Recall basic information or specific facts; remember terms, principles, theories	State, define, identify, list, recognize, recite, outline, name, select
Comprehension	Take basic information and translate, interpret, or describe it in student's own words	Compare, summarize, describe, generalize, restate, rewrite, give an example, demonstrate, estimate
Application	Transfer new information to a new situation	Manipulate, modify, use, relate, demonstrate, predict, apply, perform, solve
Analysis	Break information into its component parts	Arrange, distinguish between, discriminate, differentiate, classify, separate
Synthesis	Put information together in *new* ways	Devise, construct, assemble, generate, predict, rearrange
Evaluation	Make informed opinions, judgments, and decisions based on clear criteria	Interpret, rate, evaluate, support, appraise, defend

cognitive classification system. Four categories are included in the Gallagher and Ascher taxonomy.

Cognitive Memory. Simple memory or recognition is required to formulate an answer.
Example: Who is the president of the United States?

Convergent Thinking. Analysis and integration of information is required to respond to a question (to which there is only one answer).
Example: Which would be a better long-term value, taking a 25-year mortgage at 5 percent or a 30-year mortgage at 4.5 percent?

Divergent Thinking. Independently generated information or a new perspective is needed to answer the question. Many different responses to the question are possible.
Example: Write two different endings to the story. One should be from a liberal perspective and the other from a conservative perspective.

Evaluative Thinking. The student must exercise judgment, value, and choice to respond to the question.
Example: How can we solve our DWI problem?

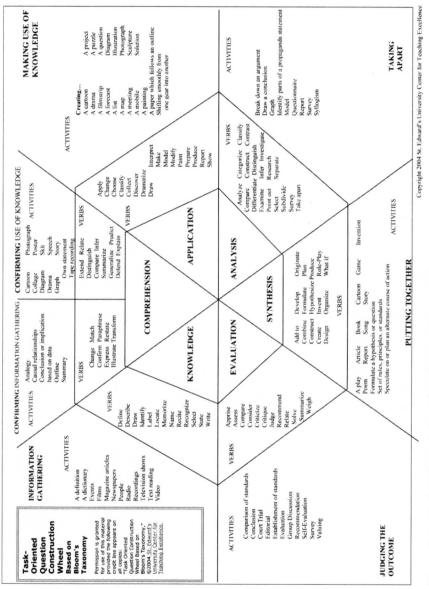

Figure 8.1 Task-Oriented Question Construction Wheel

A summary of the Gallagher and Ascher taxonomy includes:

- Cognitive memory
- Convergent thinking
- Divergent thinking
- Evaluative thinking

THE STERNBERG MODEL

Sternberg (2008), while attempting to design questions based on his model of successful intelligence—which includes analytic, creative, and practical intelligence (Sternberg, 1997)—has added wisdom to the list. He created questions not only for teaching but also for *assessing* in different subject areas. He has offered examples in all curriculum areas. The following are his questions from social studies and English:

- Social Studies (Understanding the American Civil War):

    "Compare and contrast the Civil War and the American Revolution" (*analytic*).
    "What might the United States be like today if the Civil War had not taken place?" (*creative*)
    "How has the Civil War affected, even indirectly, the kinds of rights that people have today?" (*practical*)
    "Are wars ever justified?" (*wisdom*)

- English (Understanding *Tom Sawyer*):

    "How was the childhood of Tom Sawyer similar to and different from your own childhood?" (*analytic*)
    "Write an alternate ending to the story." (*creative*)
    "What techniques did Tom Sawyer use to persuade his friends to whitewash Aunt Polly's fence?" (*practical*)
    "Is it ever justified to use such techniques of persuasion to make people do things they do not really want to do?" (*wisdom*) (Sternberg, 2008, p. 22)

Teachers can use Sternberg's examples as a guide to constructing questions in any curriculum areas. A summary of the Sternberg model includes:

- Analytic
- Creative
- Practical
- Wisdom

MARZANO'S TAXONOMY

Marzano (2001) has offered a new taxonomy of educational objectives in the cognitive domain based on Bloom's work. While acknowledging Bloom's "incredible contribution to educational theory and practice" (p. ix), Marzano claimed that in the half century that has passed since the original work in 1956, "no successful attempt has been mounted to up-date or replace the taxonomy. Yet in that same half century, understand-ing of how the mind works, the nature of knowledge, and the interaction of the two have advanced dramatically" (p. viii).

Retaining the first four levels of Bloom's taxonomy, Marzano adds metacognition and self-system thinking, a total of six levels (the same as Bloom). Metacognition is an important addition because it makes a learner aware of his or her thinking process—what his or her thoughts are and how they influence thinking. Marzano's taxonomy also describes three knowledge domains—those of information, mental, and psycho-motor procedures—each of which is operant at all six levels.

A summary of Marzano's taxonomy includes:

- Knowledge domains (information, mental, psychomotor)
- Comprehension
- Application
- Analysis
- Metacognition
- Self-system thinking

ANDERSON'S TAXONOMY

Anderson et al. (2001) have also added their voices to the need for up-dating Bloom's taxonomy. They offered four dimensions of knowledge:

factual, conceptual, procedural, and metacognitive. For each of these categories, Anderson et al. (2001) have adapted Bloom's six levels to provide a list of their own cognitive processes: remembering, understanding, applying, analyzing, evaluating, and creating.

You may have already noticed that the Anderson version has shifted the emphasis from nouns to the more active verb form. All of the expectations of students are in the gerund (-ing) form. Thus, knowledge becomes knowing, understand becomes understanding, evaluation becomes evaluating, and so forth.

A summary of Anderson's taxonomy includes:

- Knowing (factual, conceptual, procedural, metacognitive)
- Remembering
- Understanding
- Applying
- Analyzing
- Evaluating
- Creating

All these different taxonomies at first seem mind-boggling, but it is not necessary to memorize them. Regardless of the taxonomy presented,

Table 8.2. Summary of Taxonomies

Bloom	Gallagher and Ascher	Sternberg*	Marzano	Anderson
Knowledge	Cognitive Memory	Analytic	Knowledge Domains −Information −Mental −Psychomotor	Knowing (four dimensions) −Factual −Conceptual −Procedural −Metacognitive
Comprehension	Convergent Thinking	Creative	Comprehension	Remembering
Application	Divergent Thinking	Practical	Application	Understanding
Analysis	Evaluative Thinking	Wisdom	Analysis	Applying
Synthesis			Metacognition	Analyzing
Evaluation			Self-System Thinking	Evaluating Creating

* Note that Sternberg's first three attributes are not necessarily in cognitive order.

all of them (with the exception of the first three of Sternberg) classify objectives and questions from lowest to highest cognitive levels. What is important to remember when using any of the taxonomies is that they offer a way to help teachers categorize and thereby frame questions on the basis of the mental activity required from students in formulating their response.

SELF-REFLECTION

- How prepared are your students for higher-level questions?
- If your students are not prepared, how do you provide them with foundational knowledge?
- What percentage of higher-level questions do you ask?
- Are you satisfied with the cognitive level of your questions?
- Are you satisfied with the cognitive level of your students' questions?
- How can you use taxonomies to improve your questions and those of your students?

QUESTIONING FOR CRITICAL THINKING

Thinking is the hardest work there is, which is the probable reason why so few people engage in it.

—Henry Ford

WHAT IS CRITICAL THINKING?

It is highly likely that you would find stated in the curriculum goals of any school district in the United States, and perhaps throughout the world, the desire to develop critical thinking in their students. Critical thinking is a staple educational goal that has become a mantra not only for those involved in education but also among business leaders.

Critical thinking is the foundation of our communication skills—writing, reading, speaking, and listening. Social change is made possible by critical thinking. Institutions have their own assumptions that must be constantly scrutinized.

Our biases can be revealed through critical thinking. This revelation is an important step toward connecting with people different from ourselves. Critical thinking allows us to question whatever we see, hear, and read. Thus it frees us from incomplete truths and deception. On a daily basis, critical thinking allows us to evaluate every situation we confront. In essence, our quality of life is determined by how we think because we *are* what we think (Paul & Elder, 2001).

The concentration on critical thinking is now being enhanced in light of the changing economy. "Business leaders and policymakers more and more say that those higher-order, critical thinking, communication, technological, and analytic skills are the ones crucial for students to master as they enter a service-oriented, entrepreneurial, and global workplace" (Sawchuk, 2009, p. 1). However, there are those who warn that "Unless . . . all students are also taught a body of explicit, well-sequenced content, a focus on skills will not help students develop higher-order critical-thinking abilities" (Sawchuck, 2009a, p. 1).

Covering a report of the "21st Century Skills, Education and Competitiveness," Aarons (2008) wrote, "To meet the growing demand for workers who understand the information-based economy . . . the nation's education system must change from one that is focused on basic proficiency to one that encourages innovation and entrepreneurship and promotes the use of critical thinking skills" (p. 12).

The need for students to think critically and problem solve is more significant than ever considering what success will be required by the United States when competing in the global economy. President Obama, in his first address on education, called for "world-class standards" in math and science, as well as "21st century skills" such as "problem-solving and critical thinking, entrepreneurship and creativity" (Jackson, 2009).

Though there is general agreement that critical thinking should be developed in our students, there is no agreement exactly how to define it. Some see critical thinking as a deeper understanding of the written word; some see critical thinking as understanding basic facts through analyzing, synthesizing, applying, and reflecting. Others see critical thinking as a thought process having two interdependent parts: basic facts and the ability to manipulate those facts. Treffinger

(2008) sees critical thinking as synonymous with creative thinking. And Daniel T. Willingham, a psychology professor at the University of Virginia, believes that there is no such thing as critical thinking (Strauss, 2008).

Regardless of the way critical thinking is defined, it is complex. Teachers can get bogged down in arguments about the definition of critical thinking. The concept of critical thinking becomes more useful for teachers when describing what a critical thinker *does*. Teachers can then formulate questions that will elicit those activities.

The attributes of a critical thinker have been described by Ferrett (2000). A critical thinker:

Asks pertinent questions
Assesses statements and arguments
Is able to admit a lack of understanding or information
Has a sense of curiosity
Is interested in finding new solutions
Is able to clearly define a set of criteria for analyzing ideas
Is willing to examine beliefs, assumptions, and opinions and weigh them against facts
Listens carefully to others and is able to give feedback
Sees that critical thinking is a lifelong process of self-assessment
Suspends judgment until all facts have been gathered and considered
Looks for evidence to support assumptions and beliefs
Is able to adjust opinions when new facts are found
Examines problems closely
Is able to reject information that is incorrect or irrelevant. (p. 37)

Students skilled in critical thinking are thorough. They can distinguish between facts and opinions, formulate rigorous questions, identify assumptions, observe details, define terms clearly, and draw conclusions based on evidence and sound thinking.

It is obvious from all of the above that critical thinking is a daunting task. It requires that teachers be able to think critically themselves so that they will be in a better position to develop the critical-thinking process in their students.

IS THIS CRITICAL THINKING?

You almost certainly have heard comments like these in the following actual scenes:

Scene 1

Caller to a radio talk show: I don't care about tax policy because I don't pay taxes.

Radio host: Do you have income?

Caller: Yes.

Radio host: Then how can it be, how do you know that you don't pay taxes?

Caller: I get a refund every year.

Scene 2

Interviewer: For whom are you going to vote?

Responder: For _____.

Interviewer: Why did you make that choice?

Responder: Because he has a cute wife.

Scene 3

Mortgage Evaluator: Your income is not sufficient to warrant this size mortgage.

Mortgage Applicant: It will be by next week.

Mortgage Evaluator: I've checked your application and don't see anything that will be different.

Mortgage Applicant: Well, it will be because I'm going to win the lottery.

Scene 4

Consumer: I want a red Mercedes but they don't make them.

Auto Salesperson: How do you know?

Consumer: I've never seen one.

From your own experience, you can undoubtedly add many other poor thinking and inane comments like those in the above. What is particularly distressing is that this type of thinking is and has been all too common and is certainly far from the critical thinking you want to foster in your students.

One of the reasons that critical thinking is so elusive is that humans are dominated by a tendency to think and feel egocentrically. When people believe uncritically what they were taught to believe, they unconsciously use egocentric standards to justify their beliefs (Paul & Elder, 2001, 2009). These authors offer five attitudes we should examine to see how our thinking serves our egocentric agendas and how we can open our thoughts to develop rational fair-mindedness.

> *"It's true because I believe it."* . . . we often find ourselves assuming that others are correct when they agree with us and incorrect when they do not . . . we egocentrically assume we have a unique insight into the *truth*.
>
> *"It's true because we believe it."* . . . we egocentrically assume that the groups to which we belong have a unique insight into the *truth*. Our religion, our country, our friends are special and better.
>
> *"It's true because I want to believe it."* . . . we more readily believe what coincides with what we egocentrically want to believe, even to the point of absurdity. [It also follows that I do not believe it because I do not want to believe it; addition added.]
>
> *"It's true because I have always believed it"* . . . we more readily believe what coincides with beliefs we have long held. We egocentrically assume the rightness of our early beliefs.
>
> *"It's true because it is in my selfish interest to believe it."* . . . we more readily believe what coincides with beliefs that . . . serve to advance our wealth, power, or position even if they conflict with the ethical principles that we insist we hold. (Paul & Elder, 2001, pp. 39–40)

Moreover, we hold these five attitudes without ever questioning their validity. In light of the above, you should note that American writer Gwendolyn Brooks said, "Be careful what you swallow. Chew."

An example of the first attitude often occurs when a person wants to sell a personal possession, especially a house. He will often put an unrealistic price on it because he probably has a personal (egocentric) affinity to it. However, it is the market that will determine the actual price of the house no matter what the owner thinks it is worth. It is interesting to note that the Talmud says, "We don't see the things the way they are. We see things the way *we* are."

Regarding the second attitude, when we believe something without questioning that belief, this situation leads to a "group think" mentality. World War II General George S. Patton warned, "If everyone is thinking alike, then somebody isn't thinking."

Wanting to believe something, regardless of the evidence, can be detrimental, such as wanting to believe that a person can change the one she marries. It is equally detrimental *not* wanting to believe that an uncontrolled national debt will lead to insolvency and a financial catastrophe.

Voting for a political party because a person has always voted that way or buying a car because he has always owned one does not call into question what new evidence may have come into play.

And voting for a particular party because that party supports what may benefit a person instead of what may benefit the country is an example of how selfish interests can interfere with other more important considerations.

As a prerequisite for studying any (controversial) topic, it is important for you to analyze your own thinking about that topic and have your developmentally appropriate students analyze their thinking about it according to the above five attitudes.

Possible questions for this analysis could include:

"What do you believe about (a developmentally relevant topic)?"
"How long have you believed it?"
"Why do you think that you believe it?"
"What do your friends (peers) believe about it?"
"Did you ever question your belief? If so, what caused you to do so? If not, why not?"
"What evidence do you have to support your belief?"
"What evidence is there that does not support your belief?"
"How would it affect you if you did not hold that belief?"
"What do other people believe about it?"
"Why might they believe it or want to believe it?"

WHAT CRITICAL THINKING IS NOT

Before continuing with a discussion of critical thinking, it would be useful to determine what it is not. Critical thinking is not emotionless thinking. Our emotions frequently guide us to make good decisions.

Given the decision on whether or not to marry someone, a person may have all the traditionally accepted "positives" for a mate—personality, looks, intelligence, integrity, a sense of humor, high income, similar social status, and so forth—but may not connect emotionally with the other person. In short, there is no dynamism, spark, or feeling of enthusiasm or connectedness. Everything is right, but everything is wrong. Therefore, pursuing a permanent relationship with that other person might end up being disastrous.

Yet, Sylwester (2003) warns that our emotions often determine what facts we will choose to note or avoid. This point is especially important in critical thinking where openness to information is crucial in understanding problems and making decisions.

While critical thinking includes problem solving, critical thinking is not merely problem solving but goes beyond it. Critical thinking addresses larger issues, usually those having long-term effects.

Another way critical thinking goes beyond problem solving is in the realm of asking questions. Questions are a fundamental part of critical thinking, and one of the most difficult skills in critical thinking is learning to notice that there is a question you should be asking, a problem you should be solving. In problem solving, on the other hand, someone gives you the problem—and your job is to solve it. Critical thinking is different because it begins with posing the problem in the first place (Nosich, 2009, p. 18).

Table 9.1. Examples of Problem Solving and Critical Thinking

Problem Solving	Critical Thinking
Solving a quadratic equation	Deciding whether or not to pursue a career involving mathematics
Deciding which bread to buy	Planning a healthy lifestyle
Purchasing an airline ticket	Deciding which countries would expose oneself to studying art (evolution, ecology, etc.)
Should I go out with Jim/Jane tonight?	Should I marry Jim/Jane?

But, in another perspective, it has been pointed out that critical thinking is needed for problem solving. "Problem solving is a major use of critical thinking and critical thinking is a major tool in problem solving (and therefore that the two are best treated in conjunction rather than in disjunction" (Paul & Elder, 1999, p. vii).

Critical thinking is not negativity. The word *critical* often implies being a critic or being against something. Critical has its roots in "criteria," which implies that critical thinking is conducted with high standards.

Critical thinking is not learning how to think but how to think *well* (Nosich, 2009). This means that critical thinking must be practiced. "Until thinking skills become overlearned and relatively automatic, they are not likely to be transferred to new situations" (Woolfolk, 2008, p. 338).

THE BRAIN AND THINKING

It is the nature of man to think. However, if left unattended, much of man's thinking is incomplete, distorted, uninformed, and biased. Yet quality of thinking affects what man produces. Careless thinking is expensive both monetarily and in life quality. Therefore, it is critical to nurture quality of thought (Paul & Elder, 2009).

Consider how much more successful the responders in the actual situations presented at the beginning of this chapter would have been if they were better thinkers. The first responder would have been able to analyze tax policy and would have found ways to save tax and retain income so she would not have given the government an interest-free loan.

The second responder would have been able to make an intelligent voting decision more consistent with his values.

The third responder would have realized (or allowed herself to realize) that her chances of winning the lottery are about one in twelve million and would have been better prepared to consider if she was qualified to buy a house.

And the last responder might have purchased the red Mercedes, achieving a better deal not only on that car but on any other car or color he desired.

What makes it difficult for teachers in nurturing critical thought is the fact that the brain was designed not for academic work but for survival

(Alcock, 1995; Sylwester, 2003). Cognitive psychologist Daniel T. Willingham (2009) reports research indicating that thinking abstractly is not something our brains are good at or even enjoy, especially since brains are actually constructed to *save* us from having to think.

Willingham's definition of thinking is doing mental work requiring effort such as problem solving, reasoning, or reading a complex passage. He promotes the cognitive principle that "People are naturally curious, but they are not naturally good thinkers; unless the cognitive conditions are right, people will avoid thinking" (Willingham, 2009a, p. 4). He stresses that thinking is a slow, uncertain, effortful process that requires concentration, which is why many people avoid it.

Instead of thinking, we rely on memory to solve problems. Our memory system has less uncertainty than our thinking system, thereby giving us quick answers without much effort. Since most of these problems are those we have solved before, using memory makes us simply repeat what we have done in the past. Thus, when it comes to making decisions, we don't tend to pause to consider alternatives, reason about them, and anticipate their consequences.

Before you become too pessimistic about the above, be heartened by the fact that when we succeed at difficult cognitive tasks, there is a feeling of fulfillment and satisfaction. People like to think even though they are not good at it. The key for teachers is setting the conditions for thinking to thrive. One of the most important conditions is ensuring that the level of thinking is not too difficult or too easy; to gain and maintain the brain's attention, the appropriate amount of stress must be provided. Too much stress (frustration, tension) and too little stress (boredom) both tend to shut down the brain.

Think of stress as the tension on a violin or guitar string. When the string is too loose, it has no tension. If in the no-tension state the string is bowed, plucked, or strummed, there is no sound and therefore no music. But if the string is tightened too much, there is too much tension on it, and when bowed or plucked, the string will break. Given the right amount of tension, when bowed or plucked, the string will produce sound (music). In the same way, problem solving that is too hard or too easy is unpleasant and will be avoided; problem solving at the right difficulty (tension) level is rewarding and pleasant.

To understand how the brain thinks, and therefore how you can question your students to advance their thinking, reconsider the memory model in text box 9.1 that you likely studied in an introductory psychology or educational psychology course.

Text Box 9.1.   Memory Model

Sensory Memory	Working Memory	Long-Term Memory
Incoming	Location of	Location of factual
environmental	awareness and	and procedural
stimuli	thinking	knowledge

Environmental stimuli contain effects you can hear and see as well as problems to be solved. These sensory stimuli are the initial processing that converts these incoming stimuli into information from which we can make sense. Though our capacity for storing sensory stimuli in sensory memory is large, it doesn't hold these stimuli very long, most frequently between 1 and 3 seconds.

Working memory contains the content you are *currently* thinking about or are aware of. This content could include seeing lightning or hearing the sound of thunder or of a neighbor's lawn mower.

Long-term memory is the huge warehouse where you keep the factual knowledge you have acquired: a caterpillar turns into a butterfly, George Washington was the first president of the United States, the hypotenuse of a right triangle can be found by calculating the square root of the sum of the squares of its other two sides. You are not aware of this long-term information, which remains dormant until called upon to enter working memory. Then this information enters your consciousness.

Thinking occurs in working memory when information from the environment (sensory stimuli) and long-term memory are combined in new ways. Consider the riddle that you were asked to contemplate earlier. A man is afraid to go home because of the man with the mask. The environmental stimulus was the problem introduced in the riddle. You considered ways to solve the problem. In doing so, you recalled information you had stored in long-term memory about fear, home, man, and mask. The more information you had stored about "home" (a place where a baseball player returns to score as well as a place in which to reside, and a mask worn by a baseball player as well as by a robber), the better were your chances of solving the problem.

In order to be a successful thinker, you have to know *how* to combine and rearrange ideas that are in working memory. This knowledge occurs when you have experience dealing with a certain kind of problem. This experience provides you with information in long-term memory regarding how to solve the problem.

For example, when given the problem 17×9, you know how to solve it because stored in your long-term memory is relevant information. In the above case, it would be: 17 is one 10 and one 7, 9×7, and 9×1, understanding that the 1 is actually a 10. You also have stored the process (procedural knowledge) for solving this problem. First you multiply the ones and then you multiply the tens. Then you make sure you place the ones under the ones and the tens under the tens.

You have also stored many other processes such as driving to the local supermarket, cooking your favorite recipe, or opening and saving a file on your word processor.

Finally, in order for thinking to take place, there must be sufficient space in working memory. When working memory becomes crowded, thinking becomes more difficult. Problems that require a series of intermittent steps would in most cases be impossible to solve in your head because the steps would take too much space in working memory.

To summarize, in order for thinking to be successful, all of the following factors must be present: information from an environmental stimulus, facts acquired in long-term memory, procedures in long-term memory, and space in working memory. Thinking is not likely to be successful if any of the four is lacking (Willingham, 2009a).

WHAT DOES BRAIN RESEARCH MEAN FOR TEACHERS?

From the above research on thinking, there are clear implications for the classroom.

Teachers must ensure that problems, questions, and any cognitive discussions are offered at the appropriate challenge level for students because these types of problems will tend to give the students pleasure.

Problems and questions at the proper challenge level are those that are easy enough to be solved yet difficult enough to take some mental effort.

Determining this challenge level is not simple. It requires attempting several different questions and testing their effectiveness. After enough experience with those that are successful, the questions that were most conducive to successful class participation should be recorded for future use. Of course, with different classes, grade levels, and subjects, the process of determining the proper challenge level of questions should be repeated.

Teachers must be certain that their students have enough background information (entry knowledge) to be able to think about and answer the questions posed. If not, teachers should teach the prerequisite information or delay the discussion of the problem or question until students have acquired that knowledge.

Consider the point made by Ravitch (2009):

> For over a century we have numbed the brains of teachers with endless blather about process and abstract thinking skills. We have taught them about graphic organizers and Venn diagrams and accountable talk, data-based decision making, rubrics, and leveled libraries. But we have ignored what matters most. We have neglected to teach them that one cannot think critically without quite a lot of knowledge to think about. Thinking critically involves comparing and contrasting and synthesizing what one has learned. And a great deal of knowledge is necessary before one can begin to reflect on its meaning and look for alternative explanations.

And research has indicated that when students were given the opportunity to explore foundational concepts before receiving explanations from the teacher and to actually contribute to the explanations, the students spent more time on the explorations and were more frequently involved at a higher cognitive level. In addition, there was a high positive correlation between the amount of time spent exploring concepts and the cognitive level of the students (Marshall & Horton, 2011).

Since students can consider only a limited amount of information at one time, teachers should not overload the students' working memories.

When asking students to consider problems and instruction that involve multiple steps, whether these problems are mathematical, logical, or new concept application, teachers should try to judge the appropriate pace for presenting this information. Memory devices such as preprepared posters or the chalkboard (smartboard, whiteboard) should be incorporated so that the information can be recalled from these instead of having to keep it in the students' current awareness (Baddeley, 2007).

It is worthwhile to invest time in developing questions that evoke the students' curiosity and interest. These questions are those to which students can relate and those the students perceive as solvable. When planning what information (objective) students should have learned by the end of a lesson, consider planning some lessons by framing key questions the students can solve along the way. This procedure will simultaneously assist students in achieving the final lesson objective (Silvia, 2008).

Instead of using techniques such as introducing problems or discrepant events to raise curiosity only at the beginning of lessons (discovery), consider having the students applying their new knowledge *after* they learn a concept or principle. For example, after the students learn that sound is a form of energy caused by vibration, let them observe a stroked tuning fork that is then placed at an angle on the surface of a shallow bowl of water. Then ask them to explain why the water splashes.

Or after learning what a pronoun is, present a paragraph without pronouns and let the students read it *out loud* to hear the monotony of the repetitive nouns. Have the students then rewrite the paragraph using pronouns, where appropriate, and reread the rewritten paragraph.

To keep the students' attention in working memory, vary the activities to keep their interest. Introducing novelty is powerful in not only gaining students' attention but also in maintaining it (Jensen, 1998).

Since all students will likely not be prepared at the same cognitive level, respect this diversity by assigning the appropriate challenge levels to these students. Be sensitive to this diversity in asking questions and offering assignments that minimize any negative self-perceptions while providing these students realistically what they need.

A summary of these techniques includes:

Prepare questions at the appropriate challenge level.
Ensure that background knowledge is attained.
Avoid overloading working memory.
Prepare (and collect tested) questions that elicit student interest.
Pose problems at the end of lessons to apply knowledge.
Vary activities.
Keep students challenged at their own levels.

FACTS AND OPINIONS

Before considering questions for critical thinking, you must be sure
that your students know the difference between facts and opinions. Not
being able to distinguish between what the facts actually are and what
students' opinions are is a major impediment to critical thinking.

A fact is a statement that can be directly observed and can be verified
as being true or false.

Example: Helen is wearing a blue blouse.

An opinion is the expression of a person's feelings, attitudes, or beliefs. These are neither true nor false, merely statements of a point of
view, and as such, may or may not be verifiable.

Example: Helen's blouse is pretty.

Too often, opinions are stated as and confused with facts. When this
occurs, decision errors can result because opinions are subjective and
therefore cannot be verified or necessarily provide information that
holds up under scrutiny. Some of the errors produced by confusing
opinions with facts can be disastrous. Daniel Patrick Moynihan, the
late sociologist and former senator from New York, warned, "You are
entitled to your own opinions but not your own facts."

An inference is a logical conclusion (deduction) or a legitimate implication that is founded on factual information. Example:

Factual information: Helen's blouse is made of silk, is lined, and has
    extensive beading, embroidery, and hand-stitched seams.
Legitimate implication (logical conclusion): The blouse is expensive.

Before designing critical thinking questions, it would also be beneficial to reflect upon the fact that mental products and processes have natural language terms. These terms include verbs and nouns such as, but not limited to, predict, hypothesize, estimate, theorize, estimate, compute, alternatives, and evidence.

These rich thinking terms should be used daily in the classroom even with younger students. Besides explaining to students at their own cognitive levels what these words mean and giving examples, these terms, when *used in context* frequently enough, will develop deeper meaning and eventually become second nature to students.

Example: Instead of saying, "What is your opinion of Roy's recommendation?" it would be more meaningful to say, "What *evidence* can you provide to support or challenge Roy's recommendation?"

In addition, students learn to think more deeply and achieve more when they are involved in discussions that are analytic and interpretive as opposed to descriptive. It is more productive to ask students to offer reasons, defend a claim, or evaluate evidence than it is to have them define a term (Palinscar, 1998).

With this background in mind, you can proceed to consider critical thinking questions by recalling what critical thinkers do. They distinguish between fact and opinion, ask questions, make detailed observations, uncover assumptions and define their terms, and make assertions based on sound logic and solid evidence (Ellis et al., 2009).

To simplify this complex process, it is constructive to synthesize the content of the above critical thinking skills into three categories. You will note that the categories reflect all levels of Bloom's taxonomy and the taxonomies of others (chapter 8).

1. Ask questions that state, define, and clarify problems
2. Answer these questions (reasoning them out) by acquiring and evaluating information related to the problem, and
3. Be satisfied with the results so that conclusions can be drawn (Nosich, 2009).

These categories can serve as a framework for teachers in asking critical questions. Therefore, you can use the following *general* or *possible* critical thinking questions in the three categories as a guide to constructing your own questions:

Table 9.2. Questions in Three Critical-Thinking Categories

I. Clarifying the Problem	II. Obtaining and Evaluating Information Related to the Problem	III. Drawing Satisfactory Conclusions
What are the central issues involved in this problem?	From what sources can you get reliable information?	How can you be confident that you have collected enough information?
How is this problem similar to and different from other problems we have studied?	How consistent is this information?	What conclusions can we draw from this information?
What information will you need that would help solve the problem?	What information is fact and what is opinion?	What consequences might result if we made this decision?
What questions would you ask to better understand the problem?	What biases may be in this information?	
What terms (concepts) in the problem must be clarified?	What agendas may people have who are supplying this information?	
What assumptions are implied in this problem?	How can you verify this information?	
	Which facts conflict with (or verify) your opinions?	

The quality of the questions you frame at these levels is extremely important. Peak performance authority Anthony Robbins reminds us that "Quality questions create a quality life. Successful people ask better questions, and as a result, they get better answers."

PLANNING INSTRUCTION FOR CRITICAL THINKING

With the emphasis on critical thinking so rampant in school district goals, you could come away with the idea that thinking was a subject in itself that could be nurtured with dosages of medication. However, critical thinking should be an integral part of *all* subjects and should be *infused* into the curriculum. John Dewey (1933) advocated that any subject, whether it is woodworking, algebra, cooking, or social studies, is intellectual in its function and therefore in its power to initiate and guide significant inquiry and reflection.

Before teaching lessons to improve critical thinking, it would be valuable to introduce some discussions to deliberately elicit thinking questions in general. You could begin by giving several *developmentally appropriate, authentic* situations that involve critical thinking and then draw from the students what questions they would ask. Then have the students put the questions into categories, outlined in table 9.2. If the students could *discover* the three critical thinking categories (clarifying the problem, obtaining and evaluating information related to the problem, and drawing satisfactory conclusions) that would be even more effective.

Situation 1: Purchasing a home: Harriet and Bill bought a house for $350,000. They took out a mortgage for $300,000 at 6-1/4 percent interest. After a year of paying the mortgage and interest, the housing market dips and their house is subsequently appraised for $210,000. Meanwhile, Bill has lost his job and the couple can no longer afford to continue to pay the expenses. If they sell the house at its current value, they will owe the bank the rest of the mortgage, which is higher than the value of the house.

Some critical questions students might offer:

"What was the minimum down payment required?"
"What were the monthly expenses?"
"What was included in considering the housing expenses?"
"What were their combined salaries?"
"What percentage of their salaries was needed to pay housing costs?"
"How much of a nest egg did they accumulate in the event of a 'rainy day'"?
"How long would that nest egg last?"
"How secure were both their positions?"
"How available were similar positions?"
"How thoroughly did the bank investigate their ability to pay the mortgage and other expenses?"

Situation 2: Selecting a college: Jane likes to swim and wanted to attend a school that has a pool. Her research led her to select Mermaid

Table 9.3. Framework for Promoting Critical Thinking in Lessons

Objectives for Problem Clarification		Objectives for Evaluating Information		Objectives for Forming Satisfactory Conclusions	
Objectives	Possible Questions	Objectives	Possible Questions	Objectives	Possible Questions
Clarify issues	What are the central issues involved? How are each of the terms in the problem used? What do these terms mean? How might others perceive their meaning? How is this situation (problem) the same as or different from other problems we have considered?	Identify what they don't know and what additional information they need	What do you already know about this topic? What would you have to find out?	Establish criteria for evaluating information	On what basis will you examine the evidence? How will you know that the criteria have been applied? What is the best evidence that made you choose this plan?
Examine assumptions	What assumptions are implied in this problem? What do you already think the solution should be? What do you at this point think might be the best solution?	Distinguish between relevant and irrelevant information	What information is critical to this problem? What information is interesting but may not be important?	Transfer information to new situations	What experiences have you had in the past that have influenced your decision-making? How is this information relevant to this situation?
Uncover thoughts, feeling, attitudes	How would you approach the problem at this point? What do you think others might believe about this problem? What might be your motive in accepting (or not accepting) any conclusions this problem may present? How have you felt in the past about it? What biases may you have in approaching the problem?	Determine where reliable information can be located	What sources would best give objective information? What may be the agendas of those sources? What sources would give different perspectives?	Recognize similarities and differences in varying situations	How would _____ interpret this information? How is this situation the same as (or different from) the prior time this problem was considered?
Raise serious questions	What questions would you ask to better understand the problem? Why was this problem raised? What do you believe about whether or not this problem should be discussed? What agendas might those who raised this problem have?	Seek evidence that supports beliefs	What sources of information would verify my opinion(s)? What leanings would those sources have?	Predict consequences	How would this work in practice? What would happen if you do not implement this plan?

Table 9.5. Abridged Objectives from a Middle School Language Arts Lesson Plan: Using Euphemisms

Usual Objectives	Critical Thinking Objectives from Framework	Possible Critical Thinking Questions
Define the word *euphemism* and pronounce it correctly	Clarify issues	When you hear the word *euphemism*, what do you think it means?
	Recognize similarities and differences	What other words we studied sound like euphemism?
	Transfer information to new situations	What do you think the connection to those words might be?
	Generate solutions	I am going to read several pairs of sentences. The first sentence will be in its original form, and the second will contain the euphemism. How do the second sentences change the original sentences?
	Determine where reliable information can be located	How could you check to see if what you thought the euphemism did to the sentence was correct?
Give an example of a euphemism and the word, phrase, or concept to which it corresponds	Uncover thoughts, feeling, and attitudes	Create your own sentences that contain euphemisms. How did the sentences you created make you feel? Write a euphemism about yourself.

Table 9.4. Abridged Objectives from Third-Grade Science Lesson Plan: Weather (Wind)

Usual Objectives	Critical Thinking Objectives from Framework	Possible Critical Thinking Questions
State that wind is moving air	Examine assumptions	What do you think wind is?
	Clarify issues	How do you feel when wind pushes against you? How can wind cause damage? How can wind be helpful?
Identify a wind vane as an instrument that measures wind direction	Transfer information to new situations	In which occupations would it be important to know wind direction? Why? What would you need to know about measuring wind?
	Identify what they don't know and explain how they could find out	How could you design an instrument that measures wind direction?
	Generate solutions	
Construct a wind vane	Determine where reliable information can be found	How could you get information about how to make a wind vane?
	Transfer information to new situations	How can wind vanes be different but still measure wind direction accurately? (Different occupations put different symbols on wind vanes. A farmer might put a rooster in the center; a fisherman might decorate the wind vane with a lobster.)
	Uncover thoughts, feelings, attitudes	What is a symbol? What symbols would different people put on wind vanes? What symbol would you put to represent yourself?

College because it had an Olympic-sized pool. Her SAT scores were just able to get her into Mermaid College. The first semester she joined the swimming team and went to numerous parties. She was still not sure what major she wanted to choose, so she enrolled in courses required for all majors. At the end of the first semester, her grades were C's and D's and she was placed on probation.

Critical questions students might ask:

"Should Jane be attending college at all?"
"What should have been other considerations besides swimming in selecting a college?"
"What possible majors might have been of interest to Jane?"
"What skills would Jane have needed to manage both the swimming and her studies?"
"How serious a student is she?"
"Would she have been better off in a community college while deciding her major?"

After students become familiar and comfortable with thinking questions in general, future lessons would then include aspects of critical thinking appropriate to different subject areas and grades. The most efficient way to foster critical thinking in lessons is to *focus on the lesson objectives (results)* because they will not only guide your assessments and learning experiences but also channel the questions you ask. When appropriate, use objectives (or equivalent ones) from table 9.3, Framework for Promoting Critical Thinking in Lessons, to direct you in transforming lessons.

Three abridged sets of objectives from lesson plans are presented here. As you read through them, think about lessons you are planning and how you can apply similar types of objectives to increase critical thinking in your students.

The first set of lesson objectives in table 9.4 is an illustration from elementary school science.

The next set of lesson objectives in table 9.5 is an illustration from middle school language arts.

The last set of lesson objectives in table 9.6 is an illustration from high school social studies.

Behavior	Questions
Seek evidence that does not support beliefs	What sources of information would challenge my opinion(s)? What leanings would those sources have?
Recognize contradictions	How does this information correspond to the stated purpose? What may be the reason this information is presented this way?
Alter opinions when new information emerges	How have you changed your opinion(s) regarding the initial problem (solution)? What information led you to change your recommendation?
Generate solutions	What is the best plan based on the evidence? How else could this plan be implemented (problem be solved)?
Evaluate solutions	What might happen if Plan A goes into effect? What might happen if Plan A does not go into effect?
Persevere in seeking solutions	What further information would you need? Whom would you consult in getting other opinions?
Analyze their arguments and those of others	On what basis did you select (reject) this solution? On what basis did others make their decision?
Summarize opposing viewpoints	What was _____'s argument in making his final proposal? What reasons did the bank give for not taking out this loan?
Demonstrate open-mindedness	What obstacles might you fact in considering this conclusion? How have you changed your mind after studying the evidence?
Demonstrate fair-mindedness	How have you given _____ a chance to present his/her case? How well have you analyzed his/her presentation?

Table 9.6. Abridged Objectives from a High School Social Studies Lesson Plan: Local and National Economies

Usual Objectives	Critical Thinking Objectives from Framework	Possible Critical Thinking Questions
Identify factors that affect a local economy	Raise serious questions	What do we need to know to study this question?
	Uncover thoughts, feelings, and attitudes	How does the geography of the location affect its industry?
	Predict consequences	Look at the map of our town. What institutions exist in our community? How much does it cost to run these institutions? How many people do they employ? What salaries and benefits do they get? What do you consider fair or not fair?
	Recognize contradictions	What do you currently believe about the businesses in our community?
		What attracts businesses to a community? What would happen if Company X moved out of our town?
		How can we reconcile the taxes on business with balancing the town budget?
Identify factors that affect a national economy	Clarify issues	How are local and national governmental structures different? How are they the same?
		How does interstate commerce affect the national economy? How does the global economy affect the national economy? How does the global economy affect the state and local economy?
	Transfer information to new situations	How are the factors that affect a local economy similar to those that affect a national economy? How are they different?
		How can we use the same tax laws nationally that we use in our town? Which would we have to change? How can we implement that change?

SELF-REFLECTION

- What is your definition of critical thinking? Ask your colleagues for their definitions, then compare and contrast your definition with theirs.
- Make a list of comments you have heard from students or colleagues that show that they are not thinking critically.
- Audio or videotape one of your lessons. Identify the critical questions you ask and those questions that can be changed to reflect critical thinking.
- What is the difference between facts and opinions? Give an example of an opinion erroneously considered to be fact that actually interfered with a person's decision making.
- Think about a lesson you recently taught. How could you adapt the objectives so that they would lead to an increase in critical thinking questions?
- Construct some critical questions of your own on the content of this chapter.

(10)

SOCRATIC QUESTIONING

Socrates believed that questioning was the only legitimate form of teaching. To him, teaching should result in deep thinking, systematic thinking, and the pursuit of truth. This kind of teaching makes Socratic questioning different from questioning per se yet intimately linked with critical thinking.

For teachers, Socratic questioning should be used to assist students in uncovering what they know and do not know, and in applying this type of questioning in their daily lives. In order to achieve these goals, teachers must model Socratic questioning for their students. To accomplish this, the teacher (leader) *only asks questions*, directs the discussion in a systematic way through the questions asked, and assists the students in probing issues and answers more deeply.

SOCRATIC QUESTIONING CATEGORIES

There are eight general categories of questions associated with Socratic questioning (Paul & Elder, 2009a). You will note that these are similar to and can be included in the three critical thinking categories you read about in chapter 9 (clarifying problems, gathering information relevant to the problem, and drawing conclusions).

Determining the Purpose

These questions lead students to understand their own goals and agendas and those of others (the teacher, school, principal, authors, classmates). Examples:

"What is your goal?"
"What are you trying to achieve?"
"What do you want to convince _____ to do?"
"Why did you propose this?"
"What other goals should you take into account?"
"What is the reason for establishing this policy?"
"Why is this opposing goal worth (or not worth) considering?"

Clarifying Problems and Issues

These types of questions allow participants to fully understand the thinking behind the question. Examples:

"Explain your question more fully."
"What other questions should you be asking?"
"How can you ask this question from a different perspective?"
"What questions should you be asking before you can address this one?"
"Why do you think that I asked the question?"
"What does that question mean?"
"What do you already know about this issue?"

Gathering Information

As already indicated in the discussion of thinking and the brain, thinking assumes that students have information stored in long-term memory. Understanding this background information allows them to better understand the thinking behind it. Examples:

"How could you check your data?"
"On what information did you base your suggestion, decision, or conclusion?"

"What additional information do you need?"
"What experiences have you had that support or contradict these data?"
"What do you think causes _____?"
"How can you be sure that you are right?"

Interpreting Information

After data have been acquired, questions of interpretation involve meaning, the drawing of inferences, and conclusions. Examples:

"What made you draw that conclusion?"
"What other conclusions could you draw?"
"What inferences does the author make in that paragraph?"
"Given all the data, what is the best solution to this problem?"
"Suppose that you compared _____ and _____; would you come to the same conclusion?"

Understanding Concepts

These questions concentrate on shaping thinking by understanding and applying ideas and concepts. Examples:

"Explain the idea you are using in your reasoning."
"Is this the appropriate concept you are using to solve the problem?"
"Can you come up with a different concept to think about the problem?"
"Explain why this problem is legal or political."
"Are you approaching this problem from a legal or political point of view?"
"Can you say that in a different way?"
"What alternatives are there?"

Checking Assumptions

Questions of assumption assist us in understanding our thinking by knowing what we take for granted. Examples:

"What are your assumptions?"
"How did you select these assumptions?"

"What would happen if you assumed _____?"
"How do these assumptions affect your point of view?"
"What assumption is _____ making in his argument?"
"How could you check that assumption?"
"What else could you assume?"
"How is this relevant to what we have been discussing?"

Understanding Implications

Questions of implication tell students where their thinking is going. Thought is complete when the most important consequences are understood. Examples:

"If you do (or don't do) what you suggest, what might be the result?"
"What might be the consequences of this decision?"
"What might be the implications of this new regulation?"
"What are you implying when you suggest that _____?"
"Why is _____ important?"

Probing Points of View

To more fully support a student's thinking process, point-of-view questions help her understand the frame of reference within which the thinking takes place. Examples:

"From what point of view have you examined this issue?"
"What other points of view should you consider?"
"What would be another way of looking at this?"
"Given the situation as it now exists, which point(s) of view would make the most sense?"
"How would _____ present this issue from his point of view?"

Summary of Socratic Questioning Categories

Determining purpose(s)
Clarifying problems/issues
Gathering information
Interpreting information

Understanding concepts
Checking assumptions
Understanding implications
Probing points of view

USING SOCRATIC QUESTIONING IN THE CLASSROOM

Obviously, the more background information and experience students have, the more deeply the teacher can probe with questioning. While this background is largely true of older students, Socratic dialogue can also be implemented in an intellectually honest way with those who are younger. It is a matter of choosing an appropriate topic.

When introducing Socratic questioning to students, Paul and Elder (2009a) advise that you do the following:

Construct a list of questions around a central concept you want the students to learn. Advanced thoughtful teacher preparation is most essential here.

Inform the students that you are going to attempt a new questioning method and to be patient with it because you are new at this and need their help.

Explain the rules. You will only ask questions and are not permitted to answer any questions except by asking additional questions.

Inform the students that their role is to try to answer your questions.

Take your time and think out loud while conducting the questioning. Be sure to base your questions on each student's last response.

Take seriously all answers, clarifying and summarizing them to enhance understanding.

With respect to the first suggestion, Paul and Elder (2009a) offer constructed questions a teacher could list for younger students involving the concept (theme) of friends. They include several of the categories that should be reflected in Socratic questioning. Note that this list is a starting point that in no way indicates that it should be followed rigidly or even consecutively.

There is so much spontaneity in the classroom that you do not know where any discussion may lead. However, going through the process of listing possible questions will help you seize the opportunity to guide the discussion, especially when a student's answer can be probed more deeply through one of these prepared questions.

Since younger students would have had the *experiential background* (in long-term memory) to answer the following list of questions, they would be appropriate for students in second, third, or fourth grade. With adjustments, older students could also get involved in a discussion of the same topic—friends.

As you read the list, observe that the yes-no questions recommended in chapter 4 that you should avoid are in this case used to lead to responses that can be explored with more probing questions.

What does it mean to be a friend?
How do you know when someone is your friend?
Can someone be nice to you and not be your friend?
Can someone tell you things you might not want to hear and still be your friend?
Is it possible for someone to not play with (associate with) you and still be your friend?
What is the difference between a friend and a classmate?
Can your parent be your friend?
Is it important to have friends?
If someone is not your friend, how should you treat him or her?
Is it possible to be friendless?
How would you feel if you were friendless?
Have you ever refused to be someone's friend when s/he wanted you to be?
What is the difference between a friend and an enemy?
Is it possible for someone to try to injure you and still be your friend? (Paul & Elder, 2009a, p.53)

Given the above set of prepared questions and assuming that the students have been informed of the process involved in Socratic questioning, review the abbreviated script that follows to see how the questioning might actually unfold in a third-grade classroom. You will see that some of the questions on the list are implemented and additional ones are interjected as the questioning proceeds.

START A NEW COLUMN!

RG: Call it what?

THE FOUR'S COLUMN

RG: Call it out to me; what do I write?

ONE, ZERO, ZERO

(I write "100 four" under the other numbers.)

RG: Next?

ONE, ZERO, ONE

I write "101 five"

RG: Now let's add one more to it to get six. But be careful. (I point to the 1 in the one's column and ask) if we add 1 to 1, we can't write "2," we can only write zero in this column, so we need to carry _____?

ONE

RG: And we get?

ONE, ONE, ZERO

RG: Why is this six? What is it made of? (I point to columns, which I had been labeling at the top with the word "one," "two," and "four" as they had called out the names of them.)

a "FOUR" and a "TWO"

RG: Which is _____?

SIX

RG: Next? Seven?

ONE, ONE, ONE

I write "111 seven"

RG: Out of numerals again. Eight?

NEW COLUMN; ONE, ZERO, ZERO, ZERO

I write "1000 eight"

(We do a couple more and I continue to write them one under the other with the word next to each number, so we have:)

0 zero

1 one

10 two

11 three

100 four

101 five

110 six

111 seven

1000 eight

1001 nine

1010 ten

RG: So now, how many numbers do you think you can write with a one and a zero?

MEGA-ZILLIONS / ALL OF THEM

RG: So who uses this stuff?

NOBODY/ ALIENS

RG: No, I think you guys use this stuff every day. When do you use it?

NO WE DON'T

RG: Yes, you do. Any ideas where?

NO

RG: (I walk over to the light switch and, pointing to it, ask:) What is this?

A SWITCH

RG: (I flip it off and on a few times.) How many positions does it have?

TWO

RG: What could you call these positions?

ON AND OFF / UP AND DOWN

RG: If you were going to give them numbers what would you call them?

ONE AND TWO

[one student] OH!! ZERO AND ONE!

[other kids then:] OH, YEAH!

RICK GARLIKOV'S VIEWS ABOUT THIS WHOLE EPISODE

Students do not get bored or lose concentration if they are actively participating. Almost all of these children participated the whole time, often calling out in unison or one after another. If necessary, I could have asked if anyone thought some answer might be wrong, or if anyone agreed with a particular answer. You get extra mileage out of a given question that way. I did not have to do that here. Their answers were almost all immediate and very good. If necessary, you can also call on particular students; if they don't know, other students will bail them out. Calling on someone in a nonthreatening way tends to activate others who might otherwise remain silent. That was not a problem with these kids. Remember, this was not a "gifted" class. It was a normal suburban third grade in which two teachers had said only a few students would be able to understand the ideas. The topic was "twos," but I think they learned just as much about the "tens" they had been using and not really understanding.

This method takes a lot of energy and concentration when you are doing it fast, the way I like to do it when beginning a new topic. A teacher cannot do this for every topic or all day long, at least not the first time one teaches particular topics this way. It takes a lot of preparation, and a lot of thought. When it goes well, as this did, it is so exciting for both the students and the teacher that it is difficult to stay at that peak and pace or to change gears or topics. When it does not go as well, it is very taxing trying to figure out what you need to modify or what you need to say. I practiced this particular sequence of questioning a little bit one time with a first-grade teacher. I found a flaw in my sequence of questions. I had to figure out how to correct that. I had time to prepare this particular lesson; I am not a teacher but a volunteer; and I am not a mathematician. I came to the school just to do this topic that one period. I did this fast. I personally like to do new topics fast originally and then revisit them periodically at a more leisurely pace as you get to other ideas or circumstances that apply to, or make use of, them. As you revisit, you fine-tune.

The chief benefits of this method are that it excites students' curiosity and arouses their thinking, rather than stifling it. It also makes teaching more interesting, because most of the time, you learn more from the students—or by what they make you think of—than what you knew going into the class. Each group of students is just enough different that it makes it stimulating. It is a very efficient teaching method, because the first time through tends to cover the topic very thoroughly, in terms of their understanding it. It is more efficient for their learning than lecturing to them is, though, of course, a teacher can lecture in less time.

It gives constant feedback and thus allows monitoring of the students' understanding as you go. So you know what problems and misunderstandings or lack of understandings you need to address as you are presenting the material. You do not need to wait to give a quiz or exam; the whole thing is one big quiz as you go, though a quiz whose point is teaching, not grading. Though, to repeat, this is teaching by stimulating students' thinking in certain focused areas, in order to draw ideas out of them; it is not "teaching" by pushing ideas into students that they may or may not be able to absorb or assimilate. Further, by quizzing and monitoring their understanding as you go along, you have the time and opportunity to correct misunderstandings or someone's being lost at the immediate time, not at the end of six weeks when it is usually too late to try to "go back" over the material. And in some cases their ideas will jump ahead to new material so that you can meaningfully talk about some of it "out of (your!) order" (but in an order relevant to them). Or you can tell them you will get to exactly that in a little while and will answer their question then. Or suggest they might want to think about it between now and then to see whether they can figure it out for themselves first. There are all kinds of options, but at least you know the material is "live" for them, which it is not always when you are lecturing or just telling them things or they are passively and dutifully reading or doing worksheets or listening without thinking.

If you can get the right questions in the right sequence, kids in the whole intellectual spectrum in a normal class can go at about the same pace without being bored; and they can "feed off" each other's answers.

Gifted kids may have additional insights they may or may not share at the time but will tend to reflect on later. This brings up the issue of teacher expectations. From what I have read about the supposed sin of tracking, one of the main complaints is that the students who are not in the "top" group have lower expectations of themselves and they get teachers who expect little of them and who teach them in boring ways because of it. So tracking becomes a self-fulfilling prophecy about a kid's educability; it becomes dooming. That is a problem, not with tracking as such, but with teacher expectations of students (and their ability to teach). These kids were not tracked, and yet they would never have been exposed to anything like this by most of the teachers in that school, because most felt the way the two did whose expectations I reported. Most felt the kids would not be capable enough and certainly not in the afternoon, on a Friday near the end of the school year yet. One of the problems with not tracking is that many teachers have almost as low expectations of, and plans for, students grouped heterogeneously as they do with non-high-end tracked students. The point is to try to stimulate and challenge all students as much as possible. The Socratic method is an excellent way to do that. It works for any topics or any parts of topics that have any logical natures at all. It does not work for unrelated facts or for explaining conventions, such as the sounds of letters or the capitals of states whose capitals are more the result of historical accident than logical selection.

Of course, you will notice these questions are very specific, and as logically leading as possible. That is part of the point of the method. Not just any question will do, particularly not broad, very open-ended questions, like "What is arithmetic?" or "How would you design an arithmetic problem with only two numbers?" (or if you are trying to teach them about why tall trees do not fall over when the wind blows, "What is a tree?"). Students have nothing in particular to focus on when you ask such questions, and few come up with any sort of interesting answer.

And it forces the teacher to think about the logic of a topic and how to make it most easily assimilated. In tandem with that, the teacher has to try to understand at what level the students are and what prior knowledge they may have that will help them assimilate what the teacher wants them to learn. It emphasizes student understanding, rather than teacher presentation; student intake, interpretation, and "construction," rather than teacher output. And the point of education is that the students are helped most efficiently to learn by a teacher, not that a teacher make the finest apparent presentation, regardless of what students might be learning or not learning. I was fortunate in this class that students already understood the difference between numbers and numerals, or I would have had to teach that by questions also. And it was an added help that they had already learned Roman numerals. It was also most fortunate that these students did not take very many, if any, wrong turns or have any firmly entrenched erroneous ideas that would have taken much effort to show to be mistaken.

I took a shortcut in question 15 (starting with zero: "What are they?") although I did not have to; but I did it because I thought their answers to questions 13 and 14 showed an understanding that "0" was a numeral, and I didn't want to spend time in this particular lesson trying to get them to see where "0" best fit with regard to order. If they had said there were only nine numerals and said they were 1–9, then you could ask how they could write ten numerically using only those nine, and they would quickly come to see they needed to add "0" to their list of numerals.

These are the four critical points about the questions: (1) They must be interesting or intriguing to the students; they must lead by (2) incremental and (3) logical steps (from the students' prior knowledge or understanding) in order to be readily answered and, at some point, seen to be evidence toward a conclusion, not just individual, isolated points; and (4) they must be designed to get the student to see particular points. You are essentially trying to get students to use their own logic and therefore see, by their own reflections on your questions, either the good new ideas or the obviously erroneous ideas that are the consequences of their established ideas, knowledge, or beliefs. Therefore you have to know or to be able to find out what the students' ideas and beliefs are. You cannot ask just any question or start just anywhere.

It is crucial to understand the difference between "logically" leading questions and "psychologically" leading questions. Logically leading questions require understanding of the concepts and principles involved in order to be answered correctly; psychologically leading questions can be answered by students' keying in on clues other than the logic of the content. Question 39 (back to our two-fingered alien's arithmetic) is psychologically leading, since I did not want to cover in this lesson the concept of value representation but just wanted to use "columnar-place" value, so I psychologically led them into saying "Start another column" rather than getting them to see the reasoning behind columnar place as merely one form of value representation. I wanted them to see how to use columnar place-value logically without trying here to get them to totally understand its logic. (A common form of value representation that is not "place" value is color value in poker chips, where colors determine the value of the individual chips in ways similar to how columnar place does it in writing. For example, if white chips are worth "one" unit and blue chips are worth "ten" units, four blue chips and three white chips is the same value as a 4 written in the tens column and a 3 written in the ones column for almost the same reasons.)

For the Socratic method to work as a teaching tool and not just as a magic trick to get kids to give right answers with no real understanding, it is crucial that the important questions in the sequence must be logically leading rather than psychologically leading. There is no magic formula for doing this, but one of the tests for determining whether you have likely done it is to try to see whether leaving out some key steps still allows people to give correct answers to things they are not likely to really understand. Further, in the case of binary numbers, I found that when you used this sequence of questions with impatient or math-phobic adults who didn't want to have to think but just wanted you to "get to the point," they could not correctly answer very far into even the above sequence. That leads me to believe that answering most of these questions correctly requires understanding of the topic rather than picking up some "external" sorts of clues in order to just guess correctly. Plus, generally when one uses the Socratic method, it tends to become pretty clear when people get lost and are either mistaken or just guessing. Their demeanor tends to change when they are guessing, and they answer with a questioning tone in their voice. Further, when they are logically understanding as they go, they tend to say out loud insights they have or reasons they have for their answers. When they are just guessing, they tend to just give short answers with almost no comment or enthusiasm. They don't tend to want to sustain the activity.

Finally, two of the interesting side benefits of using the Socratic method are that it gives the students a chance to experience the attendant joy and excitement of discovering often complex ideas on their own. And it gives teachers a chance to learn how much more inventive and bright a great many more students are than usually appear to be when they are primarily passive.

(Used with permission: C. F. Garlikov, http//www.garlikov.com/ Soc_Meth.html.)

WHAT DO YOU THINK ABOUT SOCRATIC QUESTIONING?

Educators have differing opinions regarding the use of Socratic questioning in the classroom. Snyder (2009) revisited these differing Socratic questioning opinions by calling attention to their September 1984 issue of *Educational Leadership*, whose theme was "Thinking Skills in the Curriculum." In that issue, Goldman (1984) said:

> The Socratic method, by searching for hidden assumptions or hypotheses for any apparent *given* [italics in original], tell us that things are not always what they seem to be, that truth may not be in conventional wisdom, that matters of fact need to be transcended to discover the facts of the matter. But more than that, recognizing that an illusion is an illusion gives us no assurance that its contrary will in turn be the ultimate truth. (Goldman, 1984, p. 59)

He goes on to say that educators must provide a firm foundation in the nature and values of our culture. Without this grounding we put young people at a disadvantage and threaten the continuity of our society. Yet, lest we be accused of indoctrination, we must give good reasons for the standards our culture provides.

Socratic questioning, as it persistently searches for better options, undoubtedly leads to further questioning. Though Socratic questioning constantly provides instant relearning and reorganization of information, there is no guarantee where this questioning may lead. Thus, stability is imperiled particularly for younger students because it teaches them to question adult authority prior to having the necessary experience to indulge in this kind of questioning. Plato himself, a disciple of Socrates, suggested that Socratic questioning not be used until students had reached age 30 and had mastered all of higher education.

On the other hand, Paul (1984) states evidence that:

Our capacity to command our cognitive and affective processes is heavily influenced by the character of our early lives, both at home and school. Very special preparation is necessary if we want children to develop into adults who are comfortable with and skilled in weighing, reconciling, and assessing contradictory arguments and points of view through dialogue, discussion, and debate. (Paul, 1984, p. 6)

He believes that if students do not have the ability to reason dialectically (Socratically), they are intellectually, emotionally, and morally incomplete. Paul distinguishes between two kinds of problems—those faced in the technical domains and those real-world problems that are logically messy.

Closed systems of ideas and procedures are used to solve the technical problems, but it is rare to solve in a rational manner problems encountered in everyday life because they are rife with opposing viewpoints, contradictory methods of reasoning, and the realities of self-delusion and power.

To the extent that schools have addressed problem solving at all, it has been in the realm of technical problems with their concomitant technical reasoning. The result has been using technical reasoning for solving everyday problems illicitly, or tacitly instilling the students with preconceived answers of the dominant social majority or of some favored minority.

To ensure that this inculcation does not occur, Paul (1984) recommends the teaching of affective and logical analytic critical (cognitive) thinking skills. He also proposes the teaching of critical or analytic vocabulary. Such terms would include assumption, inference, credible, doubtful, premise, conclusion, reason, fact, problem, question at issue, evidence, interpretation, and other similar thinking words.

Further, he states that one of the obstacles to developing critical thinking is the failure to recognize that much of our thinking is subconscious, irrational, and automated. One of the ways to remove this obstacle is through employing the distinctive nature and importance of dialectical issues and the way they can be used in the school curriculum (Paul, 1984).

There is no doubt that teaching critical thinking and asking the questions that support it are most challenging. However, be encouraged by

the fact that Strauss (2008) reported that Michael Tabachnick, professor of physics at Delaware Valley College in Doylestown, Pennsylvania,
who teaches a course in critical thinking, has said, "The easiest way to
encourage critical thinking is to force [students] to question everything.
. . . Is it true? Is it opinion? Is it justified by fact? . . . Students eventually
learn to analyze. Some will do it better than others, but you can always
get them to at least question."

SELF-REFLECTION

- Now that you have read examples of Socratic questioning and differing points of view regarding Socratic questioning and its use,
what do you think about its value in developing students' ability to
think critically?
- Do you use this method already? If not, are you willing to try it with
your students?
- Construct your own questions within the eight categories of Socratic questioning for a topic you have recently covered.
- For what subjects and grade levels do you think that Socratic questioning would be most appropriate?

11

CRITICAL QUESTIONING TO EVALUATE THE VALIDITY OF INFORMATION

It would be a very good thing if every trick could receive some short and obviously appropriate name, so that when a man used this or that particular trick, he could at once be reproved for it.

—Arthur Schopenhauer

We are constantly being bombarded with information. Much of it resonates, whether it is accurate or not. Unfortunately, poor decisions are frequently made on the basis of inaccurate information. To complicate the decision-making process, Alcock (1995) informs us that we are entangled in intuition, distorted perceptions, and fallible memory, and cannot routinely trust out perceptions and memories. Our emotional needs and figments of our imagination frequently supplant or interfere with the perception of truth and reality.

Alcock (1995) goes on to warn us that through teaching and encouraging critical thinking we can learn to become less irrational but will never be able to completely eradicate irrational tendencies. With this burden and challenge in mind, we must relentlessly continue to pursue clear and rational thinking in our students.

To assist students in becoming critical thinkers so that they will make accurate decisions, this chapter identifies and explains many of the techniques (tricks) that attempt to influence thought and action. Then students can begin to consider what questions they should ask regarding the information offered in these techniques. Questions should come from the three critical thinking strategies discussed in chapter 9: clarifying the problem, obtaining and evaluating information related to the problem, and drawing satisfactory conclusions based on that information.

At first, the number of these techniques can seem overwhelming. But after students are exposed to them and learn to recognize these propaganda tricks in everyday life, their identification will become a matter of routine.

Once these techniques have been studied, teachers should collect and analyze additional examples and encourage students to collect and analyze examples on their own. Information for this chapter has been expanded from the work of Marzano (2007) and Paul and Elder (2008).

IDENTIFYING PROPAGANDA

Propaganda is information put out by an organization, government, or an individual to control what you believe so that they can promote a political, religious, or commercial cause or agenda. Propaganda's purpose is to persuade you to believe in someone or something, vote a certain way, or purchase a product. The message (statement) is concealed so you can perceive it as truth. Students should be able to recognize propaganda techniques so they can be questioned and critically analyzed. Some of these techniques are listed here.

Name-Calling

Conjuring up fear and arousing prejudice by employing negative terms to create animosity or an unfavorable opinion about a person, group, belief, or situation is referred to as name-calling. Sometimes a negative label will be associated with a person or thing as a substitute for arguing the merits of his or her idea, proposal, or belief. Opponents are attacked rather than challenged with facts that refute what is being promoted by encouraging people to focus on the name being called rather than on evidence involved in a situation. Opponents could be targeted as stupid, immoral, or undesirable in order to isolate or render them powerless before a discussion even begins. Name-calling requires a conclusion without examining evidence. Examples:

"Senator Anonymous is a *poll watcher* who constantly switches her opinions with the trends instead of holding on to her principles. How could you vote for such a weasel?" (Other words commonly used in name-calling could include flip-flopper, bird-brain, mean-spirited, racist, and ideologue.)

"The opposition is a party of 'no.'"

Critical questions: What does the name (in the name-calling) actually mean? What connection is there between the idea (proposal, belief) and the name being called? What merits might the idea (proposal, belief) have if the name being called is not considered? How is attacking this person relevant to the discussion? What incorrect (or correct) information is she or he stating? What are the sources of that information? What facts are available to support a different opinion? On what basis would you form a conclusion?

You will note that these questions and those that follow in this chapter cluster around the three critical thinking categories discussed in chapter 9: clarifying the problem, obtaining and evaluating information related to the problem, and drawing satisfactory conclusions.

Closely related to name-calling is the propaganda technique of renaming, relabeling, or repackaging, which could also call for a conclusion without examining evidence. In this technique, a message is communicated to the audience or public by substituting a euphemism for the original name, label, or event in order to mitigate its effect. For example, using the word "fee" instead of "tax" will make the imposition of a tax more acceptable or have some people acquiesce without fully understanding the implications. Other examples are calling a stock market "plunge" a stock market "adjustment," calling "genocide" a "cleansing," or a "war" a "skirmish."

This technique can also work in the reverse by exaggerating the label to make it seem more serious. For instance, reporting that an ordinary "event" was a "crisis."

Blatant (Glittering) Generalities

Using "happy words," also known as "glad words," in general statements that cannot be proved or disproved can render these words meaningless. Vague sweeping statements, slogans, or catchphrases connected with values or beliefs held by the listeners. "Fair," "honest," "good," "the greatest," "best," "empathy," "compassion," and "kind" are typical examples of these words. They are unclear, having different meanings to different audiences. Since these words say nothing, they cannot be proven true or false, but their implication is always favorable. Examples:

"If we don't do the fair thing and appropriate these funds, children will die."

"Ladies and gentlemen, it is with great pleasure that I welcome you to this most auspicious gathering. We are at the cusp of a new era of challenge and we must all rise together to meet this challenge. If we don't, we must then accept failure, which I will not let happen and neither will you."

Critical questions: What do these words actually mean? What exactly is being proposed? What are the positive and negative results of what is being proposed? What legitimate connection is there between the idea proposed or promoted and the actual meaning of the words or slogan being used? If separated from the words or slogans, what are the actual merits of the idea or proposal?

Transference

Transferring a positive symbol and the prestige it may carry to a person or an idea is transference, transferring the authority and approval something the audience respects to what the propagandist wants. Political and advertising propagandists determine what the audience cares about and then attempt to associate that message or product with that symbol. Propagandists want the person or idea they want to promote to be associated with other people or groups that already have a significant amount of trust and credibility. Examples:

Wearing a collection of awarded medals by a military person when being questioned by Congress regarding his recommendations or decisions gives that person authority.

Placing several American flags behind a candidate when she gives a speech or the wearing of a flag pin is intended to associate that candidate with patriotism.

"As I already mentioned to the CEO, it is important that we present this idea to the board. He has already consented, so we will move forward with it at the next meeting."

Critical questions: What is the person attempting to promote? Who is referred to in the testimonial? How much of an expert is this person? What other "experts" disagree with the proponent? If you removed the association with that person or symbol, would there be any value in the idea, product, or proposal? What vested interest does the proponent of the idea, product, or proposal have?

False Analogy

Assigning similarity to two things that may or may not actually be similar is a false analogy. It assumes that because two things are similar in some ways, they are similar in other or all ways. Using analogies is a powerful way to try to persuade you to translate the feelings of certainty you have about one topic to another about which you have not formed an opinion. Examples:

Comparing the Vietnam and Iraq wars.
"Children are like animals. They should be seen and not heard."

Critical questions: What are the characteristics of the first situation? How similar are these situations? What are the differences between them? What evidence can you give that would support what worked in one situation will work in another? What might be the results if we adopted (or did not adopt) this assumption?

Testimonials

This technique is the use of celebrities or respected sources to endorse a product or proposal. The propagandist hopes that if this source approves of the product or proposal, the audience will follow.

The endorsement may be only one indication of its possible value or validity. Examples:

A glamorous movie star endorses a diet product.
A general supports a military invasion.

Critical questions: Who is the respected source or celebrity touted in the testimonial? What is the source or celebrity supporting? What does this person know about this product or subject? Why should you consider this person an expert? What does he or she stand to gain by endorsing or promoting it? How do we know that this person actually uses this product? What evidence is there that this product, service, or proposal actually does what it says it does? What might be some of the negative effects of using this product? Can the product, proposal, or law stand alone on its merits without the person's endorsement? What other experts disagree with the endorsement and for what reasons?

Plain Folks

Convincing viewers to support a person or thing by showing ordinary people performing ordinary activities is another type of propaganda. These people are usually from humble origins, are trustworthy, and seem to have the viewers' interests at heart. This technique aims at having viewers identify with the "ordinary people" who are shown to use similar verbal and body language. Examples:

Showing people in the background dressed as farmers who are carrying placards supporting a farm bill being proposed in Iowa.
Having people of the same ethnic background as the target audience endorsing a product or service and speaking about it with the same accent, inflection, and mannerisms.

Critical questions: Who are the people in the ad, political rally, or other event? What would they tend to believe, act, or do? How trustworthy are they when isolated from the problem, topic, or proposal being promoted? What are the facts regarding the problem, topic, or proposal? How is your belief system the same or different from theirs?

How strong are the ideas proposed when separated from the personality of the ordinary people?

Card Stacking

Card stacking is slanting a message in the favor of the person conveying it by making the best possible case for that person and the worst for his or her opposition. Half-truths are provided by omitting key words or unfavorable statistics. Only facts that support the proponent's argument are produced, thus making it difficult for the audience to make an informed decision. Example:

A senator states that his bill will lower costs and include more people in the service he is proposing.

Critical questions: What facts are being twisted or omitted? What other arguments can support this person's assertion? What arguments can be made that do not support this person's claim? How can one reconcile lowering costs if more people are added? What other information is needed before a decision can be made?

Bandwagon

Encouraging you to join the crowd because everyone else is doing it is called "bandwagon." This technique promotes the illusion that the idea, proposal, or law has widespread support so you don't want to be the person who is left out. If you don't join, opportunity will pass you by. Not only does the bandwagon propagandist want you to join the movement, product, or proposal but wants those who have already adopted the movement to stay aboard. Examples:

"You know that everyone is for the X Amendment, so you surely want to sign this petition supporting it."

"These actresses are using this skin product, and you want to look like them."

"Your neighbors all bought this sales program and you will want to also."

Critical questions: What exactly is the proponent's program or product? What evidence supports or does not support the program or buying the product? Why should you support the program or buy the product? What will happen if you don't support it? What additional information do you need?

Either/or Fallacy

Providing you with only two choices where there may be other options is the either/or fallacy. There is no middle ground and therefore no room to discuss and negotiate. This technique is used to polarize issues. Examples:

"You pass all this budget or none of it."
"You either support health care or you don't."

Critical questions: How necessary is this budget item? What evidence can you give that these are the only options? What is the best argument for both sides? How can you take the best of both sides to create new alternatives? What other alternatives will give the same result?

Faulty Cause and Effect (If . . . Then)

Suggesting that since B follows A, A causes B is faulty cause and effect. It is also claiming that one event caused another simply because it occurred first. While two events or two sets of data may be related, it does not necessarily follow that one caused the other to occur. Examples:

People who live in a certain area have a high incidence of a particular disease, so living in that area causes the disease.
Since Chinese people eat a lot of rice and have a lower incidence of cancer, then eating rice prevents cancer.

Critical questions: How can you verify that this was the only cause of this event? What other factors could have caused this event? What might be the vested interest in the person claiming the cause?

Summary of Propaganda Techniques

Name-calling
Blatant generalities
Transference
False analogy
Testimonials
Plain folks
Card stacking
Bandwagon
Either/or fallacy
Faulty cause and effect

RECOGNIZING FAULTY LOGIC

To be effective critical thinkers, students must be able to reason well. Therefore, they should be trained to recognize faulty logic by others and themselves. In addition, if teachers are genuinely interested in not having students adopt false beliefs, then students must examine not only the logic they don't like but also *the logic of that with which they agree*. This process requires that the students stop, concentrate, and analyze statements carefully.

Teachers must be prepared to provide examples of faulty logic, preferably those from experiences the students likely have had. Then students should be encouraged to continue to be aware of and come up with their own examples and questions.

Table 11.1 presents samples of faulty logic errors along with examples and some critical questions relevant to the examples:

To develop critical thinking, students must also be able to recognize errors of attack and errors of weak reference.

Errors of Attack

Poisoning the Well   This technique is evidenced when a person is so committed to a position that he or she explains away or rationalizes everything opponents offer instead of being open-minded. Negative information about an issue is presented to an audience in advance

Table 11.1. Faulty Logic Errors

Error	Definition	Examples	Critical Questions
Contradiction	Putting forth an argument by offering information that directly opposes information within the same argument.	A person states that the budget is too inflated and must be cut. Subsequently, he places an additional item in the budget.	Which items should be eliminated in the budget? What reasons can you give to support your selection? Why is your budget item necessary? How can you reconcile your addition of this item with your position?
Accident (Hasty Generalization)	Not realizing or hiding the fact that an argument is founded on an exception to the rule, a small sample, or a biased sample.	A school district argues that it has high SAT scores because a few students have achieved perfect scores.	How many students had perfect scores? What percentage of the student body do they represent? How does this compare with the percentage of students who had perfect scores in other districts? In similar districts? How many students took the SATs? What was the average score? How does this average compare with the average in other districts? In similar districts?
False Cause (Similar to Faulty Cause and Effect)	Confusing an order of events with their cause.	Claiming that joining gangs is caused by poverty.	How many students in this community are considered to be on the poverty level? What percentage of these students are in gangs? How different is this percentage from that in other communities with the same and/or different poverty levels? What is the percentage of students in middle (or upper) class communities who have joined gangs? What other factors could have caused students to join a gang?
Begging the Question	Assuming a claim is true without any evidence besides the claim itself, thereby assuming what one claims to be proving.	Women write the best novels because men do not write novels as well.	What agencies rate novels? What criteria are used in the ratings? How do women compare with men in the ratings?

Fallacy	Description	Example	Questions
Evading the Issue	Glossing over or sidestepping a topic by changing the topic.	When challenged whether gays in the military could be troublesome, the response offers examples of gays winning combat medals for bravery.	What evidence is there that gays have been disruptive? What evidence is there that gays have not been disruptive? What percentage of gays are in the military? What percentage of gays won combat medals? What percentage of nongays have won combat medals? What does winning medals have to do with the effect of gays in the military?
Arguing from (or Appealing to) Ignorance	Arguing that a claim is true because its contradiction has not been (or cannot be) proven to be false or arguing that a claim is false because it has not been (or cannot be) proven to be true.	A parent argues that vouchers will not harm schools because no one has proven that vouchers harm schools.	What evidence is there regarding the effect of school vouchers? How does a school with a similar student population compare with schools that have or do not have vouchers?
Slippery Slope	Arguing that since the first step in a potential series of events has occurred, then the next steps in the series must be inevitable.	A politician argues that because a person uses marijuana, he or she will eventually become a heroin addict.	How long did he or she use marijuana? What other drugs might he or she have used? What other factors could have caused the move to heroin? What percentage of heroin addicts never smoked marijuana?
Composition and Division	Attributing something to a whole that is true of its parts (Composition). Attributing to all of the parts what is true about the whole (Division).	A school with high SAT scores claims its students are superior (composition). Promiscuous behavior of someone in a particular ethnic group is attributed to the behavior of all (division).	How does the percentage of students who scored in the superior range compare with those in school districts with similar populations? What percentage of people in _____ have been accused of promiscuous behavior? How is that percentage different from that in other ethnic groups?

specifically with the intension of discrediting or ridiculing that issue. Examples:

Being so against the opposite political party that the person finds all reasons to argue against their positive proposals.

"Now you all know that school vouchers have a negative effect on public schools."

Ad Hominem   Ad hominen ("to the person") is personally attacking the individual making a claim, or rejecting an argument or claim being proposed by an opponent by offering irrelevant facts about that person, thereby using these irrelevant facts to discredit his or her argument or claim. Examples:

"Before you consider my opponent's argument, remember that she was convicted for drunk driving."

"Don't pay attention to what he says. You must know that he's an adulterer."

Appealing to Force   Using threats to establish the validity of a claim is a way of appealing to force, or a type of one-sided argument whereby force or threat is used to suppress arguments on the opposite side of an issue. Example:

A union against binding arbitration might threaten a strike.

Errors of Weak Reference

Appeal to Authority   Referring to an authority as the final word on an argument or issue as opposed to exploring additional sources is an appeal to authority. Propping up a weak argument by referring to an authority figure, especially as a substitute for factual information, is typical of this. Examples:

"Scientists say that this vitamin can help prevent heart disease."

"The Congressional Budget Office report says that this project is a nonstarter."

Appeal to the People   This method is a way of justifying a claim on the basis of its popularity instead of on objective sources of data for the claim. A person might attempt to use the desire of most people to fit in and be accepted to try to get the audience to accept his argument. Examples:

Year-round school opponents claim that students would hate it.
"Smoking pot is immoral. Eighty percent of the country is against it."

Appeal to Emotion   Citing an emotional "sob story" as proof for an issue or claim as opposed to producing relevant data is using emotion as the basis of the appeal. Examples:

A politician uses the death of a child in a shooting as an argument for gun control.
"Senior citizens will have to eat dog food if this bill is passed."

Biased Sources   Accepting data supporting what one believes or wants to believe, or consistently rejecting data that do not support what one believes, are instances of biased sources. Example:

Accepting only data supporting a public health-care option because a person wants one or rejecting information that supports a public health-care option because a person does not believe in this option.

Sources That Lack Credibility   Using biased sources or those that are not reputable relies on sources that lack credibility, especially when a person wants to promote the point of view that source reflects. Example:

Citing only sources dedicated to promoting government-run health care to advance that point of view.

Summary

Errors of Attack	Errors of Weak Reference
Poisoning the well	Appeal to authority
Ad hominem	Appeal to the people
Appeal to force	Appeal to emotion
	Biased sources
	Sources that lack credibility

For a list of Web resources regarding critical thinking vs. specious arguments, go to http://www.laetusinpraesens.org/links/webcrit.php.

SELF-REFLECTION

- Add your own examples to the propaganda techniques and errors of faulty logic offered in this chapter. Construct critical questions based on those examples.
- Rewrite the errors of attack and errors of weak reference in chart form. Add your own critical thinking questions to the errors of attack and errors of weak reference.
- After discussing the content of this chapter with developmentally appropriate students, ask them to identify propaganda techniques and faulty logic errors to which they have been exposed.
- Watch a news program or interview with the specific intention of identifying propaganda and faulty logic. Ask your students to do the same. Share these with each other and ask the students to construct critical questions based on the identified techniques.
- Ask your students to construct posters identifying propaganda and faulty logic with one example of each. Have class members add examples and construct critical questions based on the propaganda and faulty logic on the posters.

(12)

IMPLEMENTING QUESTIONING SKILLS

Whoever acquires knowledge but does not practice it is as one who ploughs but does not sow.

—Saadi

In this book, you reviewed effective questioning skills you may have already studied and have also acquired new information. However, it is one thing to know about effective questioning skills and another to actually be able to implement them.

Knowledge of any teaching skill, including questioning, reaches its full potential when you can translate that knowledge into performance.

A FRAMEWORK FOR ACQUIRING TEACHING SKILLS

Learning even the most basic skills takes time; developing teaching skills is a lifelong endeavor. A framework for acquiring teaching skills was offered by Joyce and Showers (1995, 2002). This framework includes theory exploration, demonstration, practice with accompanying feedback, and adaptation and generalization.

1. Theory Exploration

As a professional, the teacher must first understand the research and guiding principles that oversee their use. You have already accomplished this knowledge by studying the prior chapters and will accomplish more when you complete the text. You can further explore skills through additional readings and discussions with colleagues.

2. Demonstration

In this phase, the skill to be improved or the new skill is modeled for the teacher. Examples of the skill in action may be conducted through written samples, a live demonstration by a peer or an outside expert, and through videotapes or computer simulations. Teachers have often complained that in their teacher education programs professors never modeled or provided adequate examples of the practices that were promoted (Reiman & Thies-Sprinthall, 1998).

3. Practice with Accompanying Feedback

It has often been said that the three most important things in real estate are location, location, and location. It can also be said that the three most important activities in developing teaching skills are practice, practice, and practice.

The role of practicing cannot be overemphasized. Practice is required to develop any skill whether it is in the arts, sports, or teaching. You can do some of the practice on your own (unit planning, constructing teacher tests, rubric construction). But when your practice session involves *interaction with students*, it should be recorded through audio or videotaping so that performance is documented.

Though you can practice and evaluate your own performance, *practice is more effective when it occurs with colleagues*. Teaching used to be a very lonely profession. When a teacher closed her door, she had to fend for herself with no input from colleagues, only an occasional observation and checklist evaluation from a supervisor or principal.

On the occasion of his retirement in 2000, John (Jack) Welch, former CEO of General Electric, communicated to his employees that whatever they could do well on their own, *they could do much smarter with others.* Teachers are now working much smarter by diagnosing students together, planning together, co-designing and selecting assessment tools and curriculum materials, observing each other, and giving one another feedback regarding performance. Peer interaction has been demonstrated as being necessary for teacher growth (Danielson, 1996).

As soon as possible after the practice session, you should receive feedback regarding your performance from your colleagues. Immediate feedback allows you to become aware of the parts of your performance that were successful and those that need adjustment. Receiving this feedback prevents poor performance from becoming routine.

When your performance is interactive in nature, microteaching—teaching a short lesson to a small group of your students, concentrating on only a few skills, usually not more than three—should be used. It is essential that the microteaching session be audio or videotaped.

Since a microteaching lesson is short and focuses on just a few skills, the teacher can specifically concentrate on developing just those particular skills and evaluating them readily. It is simple to count how many times they have appeared in the microteaching session so that subsequent microteaching sessions can document the increase of effective behaviors. Practice under microteaching conditions can then continue until the desired level of achievement has been realized.

4. Adaptation and Generalization

There is no point in developing any classroom skills if they are not actually implemented in the classroom. Once the skills have been practiced in a clinical setting with a small group of your peers or students, the skills can then be implemented with the whole class. Video or audiotaping interactive skills remains a critical necessity so that you can receive feedback for yourself and from your mentors and colleagues. In all cases, it is essential that you self-evaluate and self-reflect.

THE POWER OF COACHING RUBRICS

To assist you in self-reflection as you endeavor to improve your questioning skills and acquire new ones, you will find at the end of this chapter a personal guided observation instrument—a coaching rubric. This coaching rubric is a set of criteria for *developing* performance. The criteria in the rubric were designed collaboratively after teachers researched the topic of questioning.

Coaching rubrics do exactly what their name implies: They coach and guide your performance. They will also document your growth. Documentation is of particular consequence because it has been reported historically that there is a gap in perception between what teachers *think* they do in the classroom and what they *actually do* (Brophy & Good, 1974; Hook & Rosenshine, 1979; Sadker & Sadker, 1994; Delpit, 1995).

Besides serving to summarize important content presented throughout this book, coaching rubrics in general serve many other functions. Coaching rubrics expose teachers to best practices (mastery performance), offer a medium with which to internalize best practices, constantly remind teachers of best practices, analyze present teaching performance, compare present performance to best practices by identifying skills yet to be mastered, refine present skills, serve as tools for acquiring a new repertoire of skills, foster communication and dialogue among colleagues to continually identify excellent teaching criteria, provide a forum for discussing with colleagues better examples of criteria, provide a structure for adjusting criteria and for creating new rubrics when an innovation or new research emerges, and evaluate teaching skills after practice.

The coaching rubric will empower you to take control over your own questioning skill development immediately.

The Difference between Coaching and Scoring Rubrics

Coaching rubrics are different from scoring rubrics with which you are likely to be already familiar. Scoring rubrics are a set of criteria for *judging* performance. In a scoring rubric, the criteria (descriptors) are arranged in a hierarchy that ranges from the poorest to the best performance. A scoring rubric is holistic in that performance is either scored numerically (for example, 1–6) or verbally (such as "emerging" to "outstanding") according to a set of criteria (descriptors). Holistic rubrics assess *overall quality* of student work such as organization of a report, creativity in writing, or critical thinking. For a score to be assigned, all criteria (descriptors) have to be taken into account *simultaneously* (Brookhart, 2004). Example:

In a scoring rubric for map legends (text box 12.1), the following scores (1, 2, or 3) represent the corresponding performance levels.

Text Box 12.1.   Map Legend Scoring Rubric

Level 3 (Higher Order):   Creates an original legend to communicate spatial arrangements and directions

Level 2 (Complex):   Interprets map subtleties that go beyond just reading the legend

Level 1 (Basic):   States literal meanings of legend items (adapted from Lazear, 1998, p. 56)

You will observe in the above scoring rubric that performance levels are ranked and *all levels of performance have to be considered* before judging which score (1, 2, or 3) to assign.

In contrast, the criteria in coaching rubrics are not necessarily arranged in a hierarchy. Coaching rubrics are analytic in that each criterion (descriptor) assesses *specific aspects* of performance and is evaluated *separately* not by rating the criterion but by identifying specific examples of the criterion.

The criteria must also be specific and observable enough so that more than one person observing the performance will be able to agree if each criterion had been demonstrated. Specificity and observability give the rubric reliability (Wiggins, 2005).

Table 12.1.   Rubrics

Scoring	Coaching
Judge performance	Develop performance
Criteria arranged in a hierarchy (performance levels)	Criteria not necessarily arranged in a hierarchy
All criteria evaluated together to assign a score (holistic)	Each criterion evaluated separately (analytic)
Score (usually numerical) assigned	Specific and accurate examples of criteria must be indicated

How to Use Coaching Rubrics

Coaching rubrics are easy to complete. After experience with the first coaching rubric, teachers have often expressed how simple these rubrics are to work with and how effective they actually are in improving professional practice.

As an illustration, consider the Coaching Rubric for Professional Development in table 12.2. The criteria in this rubric were developed by teachers after studying effective practices in professional development. The rubric is filled in partially to explain how to use the Coaching Rubric for Effective Questioning, which is presented at the end of this chapter (table 12.4). Before you continue reading, examine this sample rubric, table 12.2, carefully. Viewing the rubric will provide you with a frame of reference and a context for the explanation that follows.

Table 12.2. Coaching Rubric for Professional Development (T)

Criteria (Descriptors)	Performance Indicators (Examples)
The Teacher . . .	
identified reading for personal and professional broadening	identified *Classroom Instruction That Works* By Robert Marzano et al.
read the materials and was able to describe what was learned	read text, learned that the nine major instructional strategies which affect student achievement are: identifying similarities and differences; summarizing; reinforcing effort; homework and practice; using nonlinguistic representations, cooperative learning; setting objectives; generating and testing hypotheses; using questions, cues, and advance organizers
used the new learning acquired from the materials in the classroom	used similarities and differences when teaching verbs by comparing them with other verbs and contrasting them with other parts of speech
evaluated the effect of the new learning on instruction	evaluated students on subsequent test on which they performed significantly better than they had before I made the comparisons/contrasts and just gave them definitions and examples
identified a relevant professional association (or associations)	identified the ASCD

Criteria (Descriptors)	Performance Indicators (Examples)
joined the professional association(s)	joined the ASCD in June
participated in the association's activities and can describe what was learned	
transferred the new learning acquired from the professional association to the classroom and evaluated the effect of the new learning	
identified a mentor to assist in professional development	identified veteran master teacher Marian Floyd
identified others with whom to network	identified and contacted June Larson and Roy Pinzer from neighboring districts
identified ways to act as an agent to arrange for complementing my teaching	
collaborated with colleagues to obtain feedback for self-reflection	collaborated with fellow 4th-grade teachers Lisa, Tom, and Frank
used guided observation for self-reflection	used the Coaching Rubric for Lesson Planning and Implementation with my colleagues to evaluate my videotape
sought input from learners	sought input from class every Friday in both writing and in classroom discussion regarding how well the week went and what could be done to improve instruction on the part of both the students and myself
used a self-reflective journal	used a self-reflective journal to jot down what happened each day. Arranged with Marian Floyd to discuss my journal once a week.
developed a portfolio for self-reflection	
As a result of the above, the teacher . . .	
identified own professional development needs	
devised a plan to meet the needs	
if learning/perfecting a particular skill/ model was identified as a need for development,	
explained the theory supporting the skill/ model	
if necessary,	
arranged to have the skill/model demonstrated by an expert or video simulation	
practiced the skill/model with feedback (under microteaching conditions where applicable) until a desired level of achievement was attained	
implemented that skill/model in the classroom with the whole class	
evaluated the implementation of that skill/model in the classroom with the whole class	

You will notice that the coaching rubric is divided into two columns—
Criteria (descriptors) and Performance Indicators (examples)—and
that some of the Performance Indicators are completed and others are
blank. The column on the left lists specific research-based skills (criteria) associated with a particular rubric.

Coaching rubrics represent mastery performance. When working
with coaching rubrics, you should understand from the beginning that it
is not expected, necessary, or in most cases possible that anyone can perform all the criteria in the rubric all the time (Wiggins, 1998). However,
since the criteria are determined because they positively correlate with
student achievement, implementing many of the criteria will increase
the chances for reaching all learners successfully.

As already indicated, the criteria in a coaching rubric are not necessarily listed in order. For instance, you can join a professional organization before identifying reading for personal broadening. You can identify peers with whom to work before doing either of the above.

The column on the right presents the Performance Indicators. The
teacher (colleagues, evaluators) must put in writing in this column *exactly how each criterion was actually demonstrated, providing specific,
detailed and appropriate examples*. This process provides objective and
more reliable performance data, making it easier for several observers
(peers, colleagues) to agree that the performance has actually occurred.

Documentation of the examples is more focused and precise because
the *same verb and tense* stated in the criterion are also used in the
indicator. Verbs used in the Criteria (descriptors) are expressed in the
past tense describing what the teacher actually did, *not what he or she
plans to do*. For instance, the third criterion in the Coaching Rubric for
Professional Development is "Enlisted peers with whom to collaborate."

Inappropriate ways to state the Performance Indicator would be
stating what *will* be done in that category; putting a check, writing
"Satisfied," "Completed," "Yes," or an equivalent term next to the corresponding criterion; numerically scoring the criterion; or offering an
irrelevant example. *Appropriate* ways of stating the Performance Indicator for this would be writing the names of the persons who agreed to
be collaborators next to the corresponding criterion, such as "Enlisted
(same verb and tense as the one in the criterion) Paul and Sally from my
teaching team." Otherwise, the Performance Indicator for this criterion
would remain blank.

Because the documentation is so specific, coaching rubrics are more informative than the traditional type of rubric that judges performance through rating scales where raters place a check mark for each criterion in the corresponding box.

Traditional rubrics, with scale variations (such as 1–4, 1–5, 1–7), are commonly used to evaluate teachers. However, these rubrics "don't give specific enough information . . . to use for further learning" (Brookhart, 2004, p. 77). Receiving a reported rating (score), such as 3 for Average on any scale used, although it does give some feedback, does not inform the teacher during the self-reflective process what "Average" performance actually is, nor does it guide him or her how to improve in that category.

You have already observed that there are blank spaces under Performance Indicators in the Coaching Rubric for Professional Development presented above. Spaces that are not filled provide specific feedback identifying where performance could be improved.

Though the emphasis is on demonstrating positive criteria, occasionally a rubric will list some ineffective criteria as well as those criteria to be eliminated, and will be identified as such. For example, in the Coaching Rubric for Effective Questioning presented at the end of this chapter in table 12.4, one of the ineffective criteria identified is "Reacted negatively to a student's answer either verbally or through gestures." In such cases, subsequent practice would aim at *avoiding* these ineffective practices so that the Performance Indicators should remain blank.

The first session using any rubric provides baseline data regarding performance on that rubric. From the baseline data, it can then be determined which additional criteria (descriptors) should be demonstrated or increased, and which ineffective criteria, if any are identified as such on the rubric, should be avoided in future performance. After obtaining the baseline data, the teacher can then practice, addressing only a few criteria at one time.

Table 12.3. Completing Performance Indicators for Corresponding Coaching Rubric Criteria

Correct Completion	Incorrect Completion
Use the same verb	Use a different verb
Use the same tense	Write what will be done
Provide a specific example	Provide a general or vague example
Provide a relevant example	Provide an irrelevant example
	Use terms such as "Yes," "Completed," or "Satisfied," place a check mark, or score numerically.

In their attempt to offer a teacher evaluation system that goes beyond using observation forms and changing them periodically, Danielson and McGreal (2000) have offered a blueprint with three essential attributes: the "what," the "how," and "trained evaluators." The "what" includes clear criteria for exemplary practice based on current research; the "how" involves the abilities of school districts to guarantee that teachers can demonstrate the criteria and to provide "trained evaluators" who can ensure that—regardless of who is conducting the evaluation—the judgment is consistent and therefore reliable.

Coaching rubrics fulfill all three criteria suggested by Danielson and McGreal (2000). These rubrics express criteria for mastery performance (exemplary practice); help teachers demonstrate criteria by indicating which have and which have not been evidenced by appropriate examples, thereby identifying areas needed for practice; and provide a forum for "reliable evaluations" where the teacher must indicate *and peer evaluators must agree* which specific and accurate examples of criteria were implemented during actual performance.

Moreover, in the discussions of the examples among all participants, suggestions can be offered for better examples that could have been implemented. This interaction is professionalism at its best because it is highly effective in improving instruction and growth for *all* participants (Danielson, 2007).

At a time when teaching degrees, training, and certification are being questioned as definitions of a "highly qualified" teacher, a new approach has been advocated in a longitudinal study of daylong classroom observations (Pianta, 2007). "Watching teachers in action, using systematic, validated observational approaches, allows trained observers to see very clearly what good teachers do to foster learning" (p. 11). Coaching rubrics assist teachers and their colleague observers to ensure that agreed-upon researched criteria correlated with student achievement are understood and actually implemented in the classroom.

Using the coaching rubric, you are now prepared to apply the framework for acquiring the teaching skills (Joyce & Showers, 1995, 2002) introduced earlier in this chapter: theory exploration, demonstration, practice with feedback, and adaptation and generalization. You should understand why the criteria in the coaching rubric are essential (*theory exploration*). Familiarity with the research and discussion with peers are crucial processes in assisting participants in both identifying and then internalizing the criteria.

If there is a question about any criterion that is not clear, an example of the criterion should be provided (*demonstration*). Practicing using the coaching rubric can then follow in a controlled environment.

You may recall the old adage that practice makes perfect. Wolfe (2001) reminded teachers that *practice also makes permanent*. And Vince Lombardi taught his football players that *perfect* practice makes permanent. These are the reasons that you must practice *correctly* with complete understanding of the rubric criteria and why they are important. Frequent practice is important because not all classroom events will necessarily provide you with the occasion to demonstrate each criterion and do so consistently.

When the performance is interactive in nature within a limited time frame, microteaching should be used (*practice with accompanying feedback*). As previously stated, microteaching can be conducted with a small group of your students. If you and your colleagues are satisfied with your performance, you can then implement the new skills with your entire class (*adaptation and generalization*).

Some coaching rubrics, such as one that may be developed for lesson planning, have criteria that can be demonstrated within a class period. Other coaching rubrics take a longer time to implement, such as the Professional Development rubric offered in this chapter or the implementation of a Coaching Rubric for Unit Planning. Coaching rubrics that take a longer time to implement are coded (T).

Above all, it must be clear that coaching rubrics are *dynamic*. These living documents are works in progress, guidelines whose criteria should be modified when new research develops. As more studies reveal different criteria for performance excellence and as new and validated strategies and criteria are proposed, collaborators should revise rubrics or develop new ones.

Also, it is essential to understand that a teacher can demonstrate all the criteria in the rubric and yet be ineffective. The reason is that teaching is more than the sum of its parts. There are always intangibles involved that can contribute to effective or ineffective performance.

Text Box 12.2.   Directions for Using Coaching Rubrics

1. Identify collaborators (colleagues) and ensure that you and your colleagues fully understand and agree with the rubric criteria (descriptors).
2. Rubrics that take time (T) should be checked periodically to determine progress. When performance involves interacting with students within a class period, audiotape or videotape the delivery.
3. As soon as possible after the performance, document it with colleagues by writing next to each criterion under the Performance Indicators column a specific and relevant example where you demonstrated any of the criteria. Write the indicator using the same verb and same tense stated in the criterion.
4. Identify no more than three additional criteria. Concentrate on only those criteria in subsequent performance using microteaching with audiotaping or videotaping whenever student interaction is involved.
5. Continue identifying additional criteria to be demonstrated and documenting that performance until a mutually agreed-upon level of achievement is reached.

SELF-REFLECTION

- Explain to one of your colleagues how teaching skills are acquired.
- Select some peers with whom to work. Teach them how to develop and use coaching rubrics and explain how they differ from scoring rubrics.
- Examine the Coaching Rubric for Effective Questioning in table 12.4. Discuss with your peers the criteria for effective questioning and those offered for ineffective questioning. (Remember that ineffective questioning criteria are to be avoided so that you will ensure that in your questioning practice the performance indicators for those criteria remain blank.)
- Together with your colleagues, use the Coaching Rubric for Effective Questioning, table 12.4, to analyze the questioning script that follows after the rubric. Discuss with your peers at least two other ways the same lesson objectives can be taught.

Table 12.4. Coaching Rubric for Effective Questioning

Effective Questioning Practices in Phase 1: The teacher asks a question of one or more students	
Criteria (Descriptors)	*Performance Indicators (Examples)*
The teacher . . .	
set up a supportive learning environment for student participation	
secured attention of the class before asking a question	
asked clear questions	
asked only one question at a time	
sequenced questioning properly	
phrased questions so that students did most of the talking	
paused at least 3–5 seconds before calling on students after asking a question	
called on students *after* asking the question	
called on students by name	
called on a balance of volunteers and nonvolunteers	
allowed everyone to participate at least once	
demonstrated sensitivity to cultural diversity	

Ineffective Questioning Practices in Phase 1 (those to be eliminated)	
Criteria (Descriptors)	*Performance Indicators (Examples)*
The teacher . . .	
repeated or rephrased questions immediately after asking them	
asked questions requiring yes or no answers	
asked questions requiring one-word answers	
asked questions requiring a chorus response	
answered own question(s)	
asked leading questions	

Effective Questioning Practices in Phase 3: The teacher reacts to students' answers	
Criteria (Descriptors)	*Performance Indicators (Examples)*
The teacher . . .	
ignored any called-out answers	
paused 3–5 seconds before reacting to a student's answer or asking another question	
gave some feedback to every answer	
encouraged sustained responses by appropriate use of . . . asking for further clarification of a student's response redirecting questions cuing probing	
asked a student whose answer was incorrect to repeat the correct answer offered by another student	
asked another student to repeat the question a student called on did not hear	

Table 12.4 (Continued)

Ineffective Questioning Practices in Phase 3 (those to be eliminated)	
Criteria (Descriptors)	*Performance Indicators (Examples)*
The teacher . . .	
repeated a student's answer	
answered or paraphrased correctly a student's incorrect answer when redirecting, cuing, or probing would have been more appropriate	
reacted negatively to a student's answer either verbally or through gestures	
continued to elicit responses on a topic even though enough information had already been obtained	

- Tape your own class and evaluate your questioning skills with the Coaching Rubric for Effective Questioning. After you self-reflect, secure input regarding your performance on the rubric from your colleagues.

QUESTIONING SCRIPT

Science/Music Lesson: 4th grade. A Demonstration on Pitch (Whole Class)

Entry skills: Students can state that (1) sound is caused by a vibration, and (2) vibration means moving back and forth very rapidly

Lesson objectives: Students will be able to (1) define pitch; (2) state the principle that the larger the size of a vibrating object, the lower the pitch (and the smaller the size of a vibrating object, the higher the pitch); and (3) predict pitches on melody bells.

(The class is seated around a cleared demonstration table in such a way that everyone can see.)

Teacher: Today we are going to begin to prepare some entertainment for our holiday party. We are going to learn how to play songs on musical instruments. But before we can play our songs, we first have to discover an important principle about sound. Let's see what good scientists we can be. So what are we going to learn today? (Pause) Jack.

Jack: How to be good scientists.

Teacher: That's right, and to be good scientists what do we have to discover?

Jack: An important principle about sound.

(Teacher writes on board. Objective: To discover an important scientific principle about sound)

Teacher: Tell us again what we are going to do today. (Pause) Paul.

Paul: Discover an important principle about sound.

Teacher: Good, now who can say that in a different way? (Pause) Terry.

Terry: We are going to be good scientists by discovering something important about sound.

Teacher: You worded that very well, Terry. Yesterday in our science lesson we made many different sounds. What did we say caused sound? (Pause) Lou.

Lou: Vibrations.

Teacher: Great memory, Lou. Can you tell me what the word vibration means?

Lou: It means, it means moving back and forth very quickly.

(Teacher writes two sentences on the board: Sound is caused by vibrations. Vibration means moving back and forth very quickly.

Teacher: Let's all stand up and do what Lou just said, vibrate by moving back and forth very quickly the way we did yesterday.

(The teacher models the movement to the left and right and all the students follow her lead.)

Teacher: Good work, or maybe I should say workout. (Everyone laughs including the teacher.) Now that we've all finished vibrating, you may sit down again.

(Teacher takes out a toy xylophone she left hidden under the demonstration table and places the xylophone in the middle of the table.)

Teacher: Raise your hand if you know the name of this instrument.

(Several hands go up. She waits for a few more.) Paula.

Paula: I don't remember the name of it but my baby brother has that same toy.

Teacher: Who can help Paula remember the name? (Pause) John.

John: A xylophone.

Teacher: Do you remember the name now, Paula?

Paula: Xylophone.

Teacher: You paid great attention to John's answer, Paula. That's a pretty hard word to remember, but I'm sure you'll remember it now. Where do you often see this instrument, John?

John: In a marching band.

Teacher: Great. Now, class, I'm going to make a sound on this instrument. When I make this sound I want you to tell me what is vibrating or moving back and forth very quickly.

(Teacher strikes one of the bars with the hammer. When the sound stops, she strikes the bar again.) Lisa.

Lisa: The bar . . . or maybe the hammer. I'm not sure.

Teacher: How can I tell?

Lisa: Stop one of them from vibrating and it will stop the sound.

Teacher: How can I stop these objects from vibrating?

Lisa: Put your finger on them.

Teacher: Come up, Lisa. Let's try out your idea.

(Lisa goes up to the table. The teacher strikes the bar again. It makes a sound. Lisa places her finger on the hammer. The sound continues. Lisa then places her finger on the bar. The sound stops.)

Teacher: Which was vibrating, Lisa?

Lisa: The bar.

Teacher: Let's do it again.

(Teacher repeats the above with Lisa)

Teacher: Excellent thinking, Lisa. Next, boys and girls, I'm going to make two sounds with this xylophone. Listen and tell me how these sounds are different.

(Teacher strikes a bar at one end, pauses, then strikes a bar at the other end, then pauses.) Miguel.

Miguel: One is more higher than the other.

Teacher: You have a good musical ear, Miguel. One is higher than the other. We have a name for high and low sounds. Does anyone know what that word is? (Pause) Heather.

Heather: Pitch.

Teacher: Correct, Heather.

(Teacher writes the word Pitch and its definition on the board.)

Teacher: Since you were such a good observer, Miguel, come up and point to the bar that vibrated to give us the higher pitch.

(Teacher strikes the same two bars again. Miguel points to the shorter bar. Then the teacher and Miguel repeat the striking and pointing.)

Teacher: Now, class, how is the bar that vibrated to give us the higher pitch different from the bar that vibrated to give us the lower pitch? (Pause) Alicia.

Alicia: It's shorter.

Teacher: Thumbs up if you agree, class.

(Most have thumbs up.)

Teacher: Write that on the board in a complete sentence. (Pause) Frank.

(Frank writes, The bar with the higher pitch is shorter. Teacher and class check the sentence. Teacher then puts the xylophone out of sight and takes out a *tuned* guitar.)

Teacher: I'll bet you know the name of this instrument, Paula.

Paula: A guitar.

Teacher: You remembered the name of the xylophone and now you told us the name of this instrument, also. Class, when I make a sound on this guitar, what is vibrating or moving back and forth very quickly?

(The teacher holds the guitar upright and plucks one of the strings.) Cassandra.

Cassandra: The string.

Teacher: Come up, Cassandra, and let's see if you're right. If it's vibrating, can you stop it from vibrating?

(Cassandra doesn't answer.)

Teacher: When Lisa made the bar stop vibrating, what did she do?

Cassandra: Oh, she put her finger on it.

Teacher: So how do you think you could stop the string from vibrating?

Cassandra: Put my finger on it?

Teacher: Let's see. (Teacher plucks the string, which produces a sound, and Cassandra puts her finger over the string, stopping the sound.) Thank you, Cassandra. I am now going to make two sounds with these strings. Listen and tell me how these sounds are different. (Teacher plucks the two outer strings one at a time.)

Cassandra: One is higher.

Teacher: Let's do it again, and see if you still agree that one is higher. (Teacher repeats the plucking.)

Cassandra: One is higher than the other.

Teacher: Point to the one that is higher.

(Cassandra points to the thinner string.)

Teacher: How is the string that vibrates to give us the higher pitch different from the string that vibrates to give us the lower pitch?

Cassandra: It looks thinner.

Teacher: I need a volunteer to write that on the board. (Pause) Antonio.

(Antonio writes, The thinner string is higher.)

(Teacher and class check the sentence.)

Teacher: Good job, Antonio and Cassandra, you may go back to your seats. Now I want everyone to look carefully at this one string. When I make a sound with it, what part is vibrating?

(Class looks confused.)

Teacher: How could I check it out?

(Only a few volunteer.)

Teacher: What did Lisa do?

(Most hands are now up.)

Teacher: Paul.

Paul: You could put your finger on it and see if you could stop it from vibrating.

Teacher: Come assist me, Paul. (Teacher plucks one string several times and Paul puts his finger over it in several locations to stop the vibration and the sound.) You're a helpful assistant, Paul, so observe very carefully and tell me, when I pluck this string, which part is vibrating. (Teacher plucks the same string. Paul examines the string.)

Paul: From here to here. (He points from the top of the fingerboard to the bottom.)

Teacher: Let's check. If it's vibrating all along the length, could you stop it from vibrating at any point?

Paul: Yes.

Teacher: Let's try it again.

(Teacher keeps plucking and Paul stops the sound at varying points.)

Teacher: Paul is right. The string is vibrating from the top of what we call the fingerboard to the bottom. Let's say all together the word, fingerboard.

Class: Fingerboard.

Teacher: Again.

Class: Fingerboard.

Teacher: Excellent job. Now, Paul, if I place my finger here, what part of this string is vibrating? (Teacher presses the string about two inches from the top of the fingerboard. With her other hand she then plucks the string approximately midway between her pressed finger and the bottom of the fingerboard.)

Paul: From your finger to the bottom of the fingerboard.

Teacher: Is the string vibrating from my finger to the top of the fingerboard?

Paul: I don't think so.

Teacher: How could you be sure?

Paul: (He hesitates for a while.) If you keep your finger there and pluck the string again and I press my finger between your finger and the top of the fingerboard, the string will still make a sound.

Teacher: Try it.

(The teacher keeps her finger the same distance from the top of the fingerboard, plucks the string midway between her finger and the bottom of the fingerboard. Paul places his finger on the string above the teacher's finger and the string still makes a sound.)

Paul: See, I was right.

Teacher: You were. Now I need another good observer, someone I haven't called on so far. (Several students raise their hands.) Come up, Yvette. If I place my finger here (the teacher presses her finger about four inches from the top of the fingerboard and plucks the string approximately midway between her pressed finger and the bottom of the fingerboard), what part of the string is vibrating now?

Yvette: From your finger to the bottom.

(The teacher now presses her finger about six inches from the top of the fingerboard and plucks the string approximately midway between her finger and the bottom of the fingerboard.) How about now?

Yvette: The same, from your finger to the bottom.

Teacher: As I press the string with my finger into the fingerboard and pluck between my finger and the bottom of the fingerboard, what is happening to the length of the part of the string that is vibrating?

Yvette: It's, it's getting shorter.

Teacher: As the length of the vibrating string gets shorter, class, what is happening to the pitch?

(Teacher repeats the pressing and plucking.) Raul.

Raul: It sounds higher.

Teacher: Write that on the board in a complete sentence, Raul. (He hesitates then writes, The shorter vibrating string makes a higher pitch.)

Teacher: Let's look at the board. Who can remind us what we mean by pitch? (Pause) Christine.

Christine: It's how high or low a sound is.

Teacher: Excellent, now I want all of you to read the objective on the board to yourselves. (The teacher waits.) Read the objective out loud, Jenna.

Jenna: To discover an important scientific principle about sound.

Teacher: All of you examine the three sentences your classmates wrote on the board and tell me how the size of a vibrating object affects the pitch. (Pause) Hank.

Hank: The smaller the size, the higher the pitch.

Teacher: The smaller the size of what, Hank.

Hank: The smaller…the smaller…the smaller the size of the vibrating object.

Teacher: You have discovered the principle, Hank. Write it on the board. Who can say what Hank just said in a different way? (Pause) Michelle.

Michelle: The bigger the object that vibrates, the lower the pitch.

Teacher: Write that on the board underneath Hank's sentence, Michelle.

(The teacher removes the guitar from the demonstration table.

Teacher: You were all such good scientific thinkers today that I think you're ready to learn how to play songs for our holiday party. (The teacher now places melody bells on the table.) Without ringing any of these bells, who can predict which one would have the lowest pitch.

(No response.)

Teacher: What would you be looking for to make your decision? (Pause) Roger.

(Roger doesn't answer.)

Teacher: Roger, look at the board and read the sentence that will help you decide which melody bell would have the lowest pitch.

Roger: The bigger the object that vibrates, the lower the pitch.

(Teacher places all the melody bells on their sides and mixes them up.)

Teacher: You picked the right sentence, Roger, so what will help you decide?

Roger: The one with the largest piece of metal inside.

Teacher: Come up and find it without ringing it, just measuring it. (Teacher hands Roger a tape measure. He examines all the melody bells, then selects one.)

Teacher: Hold on to this bell but don't ring it yet. What did I just tell you?

Roger: Don't ring my bell but I can hold it.

Teacher: You were a good listener, Roger, now stand on the side.

(Roger takes the bell and stands on the side.)

Teacher: Who can find the bell with the highest pitch?

(All hands go up.) Ed. (Ed comes to the demonstration table.) What will you be looking for?

Ed: The bell that's the smallest.

Teacher: Find it for us. (She hands him the tape measure and Ed selects his bell.)

Take your bell without ringing it and stand on the side next to Roger. (Ed moves to the side.)

Teacher: Let's see if you were both right so far. Ring your bell, Roger. (Roger rings his bell.) Now, Ed, ring yours. (He rings it, and it sounds an octave higher. The class seems pleased. The teacher then distributes to students who have not yet participated the remaining bells and makes the students stand in *bell size order* between Roger and Ed. Using the song guide in the melody bell box, the teacher then conducts selected songs which the students then play with their bells. After the lesson the teacher displays the xylophone, guitar, and melody bells on a table in the learning activity center. The teacher asks students to write questions about anything in the lesson they did not understand or would like to learn more about. The teacher asks students who take instrumental music lessons to bring their instruments in the next day so that demonstrations could be made regarding how the pitches on these instruments are changed. Eight coke bottles are placed in the learning activity center and some students are asked to figure out how to make pitch changes with the bottles in two different ways. Other students are asked to create their own musical instruments.

REFERENCES

Aarons, D. (2008, September 10). New skills seen essential for global competition. *Education Week*, 28(4): 12.

Albergaria-Almeida, P. (2010). Classroom questioning: Teachers' perceptions and practices. *Procedia-Social and Behavioral Sciences*, 2(2): 305–9.

Alcock, J. (1995, May–June). The belief machine. *Skeptical Inquirer*, 19(3): 14–18.

American Association of University Women. (1992). *How Schools Short-Change Girls: The AAUW Report*. Washington, DC: AAUW Educational Foundation.

American Philosophical Association. (1990). *Critical Thinking: A Statement of Expert Consensus for Purposes of Educational Assessment and Instruction.* "The Delphi Report," Committee on Pre-College Philosophy. (ERIC Doc. no. ED 315423).

Anderson, L. W., Krathwohl, D. R., Airasian, P. W., Cruikshank, K. A., Mayer, R. E., Pintrich, P. R., Raths, J., & Wittrock, M. C. (2001). *A Taxonomy for Learning, Teaching, and Assessing: A Revision of Bloom's Taxonomy of Educational Objectives*. New York: Longman.

Baddeley, A. (2007). *Working Memory, Thought, and Action*. London: Oxford University Press.

Barden, L. (1995). Effective questions and the ever-elusive higher-order question. *American Biology Teacher*, 57(7): 423–26.

Black, S. (2001). Ask me a question: How teachers use inquiry in the classroom. *American School Board Journal*, 188(5): 43–45.

Bloom, B., Englehart, M., Furst, E., Hill, W., & Krathwohl, D. (1956). *Taxonomy of Educational Objectives: The Classification of Educational Goals Handbook I, Cognitive Domain*. New York: David McKay.

Borich, G. D. (2007). *Effective Teaching Methods: Research-Based Practice*, 6th ed. Upper Saddle River, NJ: Pearson/Merrill Prentice Hall.

Brookhart, S. M. (2004). *Grading*. Upper Saddle River, NJ: Pearson Education.

Brophy, J. (1979). *Teacher Praise: A Functional Analysis*. Occasional paper no 2. East Lansing: Michigan State University, Institute for Research on Teaching.

Brophy, J., & Good, T. (1974). *Teacher-Student Relationships: Causes and Consequences*. New York: Holt, Rinehart, & Winston.

Cayanus, J. (2011). *Student Question Asking in the Classroom*. All Academic Research, www.allacademic.com (accessed May 8, 2011).

Chuska, K. R. (1995). *Improving Classroom Questions*. Bloomington, IN: Phi Delta Kappa.

Cotton, K. (2000). *The Schooling Practices That Matter Most*. Alexandria, VA: Association for Supervision and Curriculum Development.

Danielson, C. (1996). *Enhancing Professional Practice: A Framework for Teaching*. Alexandria, VA: Association for Supervision and Curriculum Development.

———. (2007). *Enhancing professional practice: A framework for teaching*, 2nd ed. Alexandria, VA: Association for Supervision and Curriculum Development.

———. (2008). *Handbook for Enhancing Professional Practice: Using the Framework for Teaching in your School*. Alexandria, VA: Association for Supervision and Curriculum Development.

Danielson, C., & McGreal, T. (2000). *Teacher evaluation to enhance professional practice*. Alexandria, VA: Association for Supervision and Curriculum Development.

Delpit, L. (1995). *Other people's children: Cultural conflict in the classroom*. New York: The New Press.

Dewey, J. (1933). *How we think: A restatement of the relation of reflective thinking to the educative process*. (Rev. ed.), Boston: D.C. Heath.

Dillon, J. (1988). *Questioning and Teaching*. New York: Teachers College Press.

Dreikurs, R. (1998). *Maintaining Sanity in the Classroom: Classroom Management Techniques*, 2nd ed. Washington, DC: Accelerated Development.

Drozynski, D., Furman, T., Ellis, J., & Guertin, L. (2010, March). Using student questions to guide earth science inquiry in middle school. *Geological Society of America*, Paper no. 49-2.

Dweck, C. (Summer, 2008). The perils and promises of praise. *Educational Leadership*, 65:30–39.

Eggen, P. D., & Kauchak, D. P. (1999). *Strategies for Teachers: Teaching Content and Thinking Skills*, 4th ed. Boston: Allyn & Bacon.

Ellis, D. (1997). *Becoming a Master Student*. Boston: Houghton Mifflin.

Ellis, D., Mancina, D., Toft, D., & McMurray, E. (2009). *Becoming a Master Student plus Web Booklet for Passages*, 12th ed. (Kindle ed.). Florence, KY: Cengage Learning.

Ferrett, S. (2000). *Peak Performance: Success in College and Beyond*. Columbus, OH: McGraw-Hill.

Frisby, B., & Martin, M. (2010, April). Instructor-student and student-student rapport in the classroom. *Communication Education*, 59(2): 146–64.

Fry, E., Fountoukidis, D., & Polk, J. (1985). *The New Reading Teacher's Book of Lists*. Englewood Cliffs, NJ: Prentice-Hall.

Gall, M., Gall, J., & Borg, W. (2003). *Educational Research: An Introduction*, 7th ed. Boston: Allyn & Bacon.

Gallagher, J., & Ascher, M. (1963). A preliminary report on analyses of classroom interaction. *Merrill-Palmer Quarterly*, 9(1): 183–94.

Garavalia, L., Hummel, J., Wiley, L., & Huitt, W. (1999). Constructing the course syllabus: Faculty and student perceptions of important syllabus components. *Journal of Excellence in College Teaching*, 10(1): 5–22.

Gardner, H. (1995, November). Reflections on multiple intelligences: Myths and messages. *Phi Delta Kappan*, 77(3): 200–209.

Goldman, L. (1984, September). Warning: The Socratic method can be dangerous. *Educational Leadership*, 42(1): 57–62.

Good, T. (1996). Teacher effects and teacher evaluation. In J. Sikula (Ed.), *Handbook of Research on Teacher Education*, pp. 617–65. New York: Macmillan.

Good, T., & Brophy, J. (1997). *Looking in Classrooms*, 7th ed. New York: Longman.

Hook, C., & Rosenshine, B. (1979). Accuracy of teacher reports of their classroom behavior. *Review of Educational Research*, 49, 1–12.

Hunkins, F. P. (1974). *Effective Questions, Effective Thinking*, 2nd ed. Needham, MA: Gordon.

Hunter, R. (2004). *Madeline Hunter's Mastery Teaching: Increasing Instructional Effectiveness in Elementary and Secondary Schools*, updated ed. Thousand Oaks, CA: Corwin Press.

Interstate New Teacher Assessment and Support Consortium. (1995). *Next Steps: Moving toward Performance-Based Licensing in Teaching*. Washington, DC: Author.

Jackson, D. (2009, March 10). *Obama Urges Education Reform*. USA Today .com.

Jensen, E. (1998). *Teaching with the Brain in Mind*. Alexandria, VA: Association for Supervision and Curriculum Development.

Johnson, B. (2008). The right way to ask questions in the classroom. *George Lucas Educational Foundation*, http://www.edutopia.org/print/6261 (accessed May 8, 2011).

Joyce, B., & Showers, B. (1995). *Student achievement through staff development*, 2nd ed. New York: Longman.

Joyce, B, & Showers, B. (2002). *Student achievement through staff development*, 3rd ed., Alexandria, VA: Association for Supervision and Curriculum Development.

King, A. (2002). Structuring peer interaction to promote high-level cognitive processing. *Theory into Practice*, 41:31–39.

King, A., & Rosenshine, B. (1993). Effects of guided cooperating questions on children's knowledge constructed. *Journal of Experimental Education*, 61(2): 27–148.

Kohn, A. (2001, September). Five reasons to stop saying "good job." *Young Children*, http://www.alfiekohn.org (accessed May 8, 2011).

Lazear, D. (1998). *The rubrics way: Using MI to assess understanding*. Tuscon, AZ: Zephyr Press.

Lee, V. E., Chen, X., & Smerdon, B. A. (1996). *The Influence of School Climate on Gender Differences in the Achievement and Engagement of Young Adolescents*. Washington, DC: American Association of University Women.

Marshall, J., & Horton, R. (2011, March). The relationship of teacher-facilitated, inquiry-based instruction to student higher-order thinking. *School Science and Mathematics*, 11(3): 93–101.

Marzano, R. J. (2001). *Designing a New Taxonomy of Educational Objectives*. Thousand Oaks, CA: Corwin Press.

———. (2007). *The Art and Science of Teaching: A Comprehensive Framework for Effective Instruction*. Alexandria, VA: Association for Supervision and Curriculum Development.

Marzano, R., Pickering, D., & Pollock, J. (2001). *Classroom Instruction That Works: Research-Based Strategies for Increasing Student Achievement*. Alexandria, VA: Association for Supervision and Curriculum Development.

Newman, R. S., & Schwager, M. T. (1993). Students' perception of the teacher and classmates in relation to reported help seeking in math class. *Elementary School Journal*, 94(1): 3–17.

Nosich, G. (2009). *Learning to think things through: A guide to critical thinking across the curriculum*, 3rd ed. Upper Saddle River, NJ: Prentice-Hall.

Oakes, J., & Lipton, M. (2003). *Teaching to Change the World*, 2nd ed. New York: McGraw-Hill.

Oliveira, A. (2010, April). Improving teacher questioning in science inquiry discussions through professional development. *Journal of Research in Science Teaching*, 47(4): 422–53.

Palinscar, A. (1998). Social constructivist perspectives on teaching and learning. In J. Spence, J. Darley, & D. Foss (Eds.), *Annual Review of Psychology*, vol. 1, 345–75. Palo Alto, CA: Annual Reviews.

Palinscar, A., & Brown, A. (1989). Classroom dialogues to promote self-regulated comprehension. In J. Brophy (Ed.), *Advances in Research on Teaching*, vol. 1, 35–67. Greenwich, CT: JAI Press.

Paul, R. (1984, September). Critical thinking: Fundamental to education for a free society. *Educational Leadership*, 42(1): 4–14.

Paul, R. W., & Elder, L. (1999). *Critical Thinking: Basic Theory and Instructional Structures*. Tomales, CA:.Foundation for Critical Thinking Press.

———. (2001). *Critical Thinking: Tools for Taking Charge of Your Learning and Your Life*. Upper Saddle River, NJ: Prentice Hall.

———. (2008). *The Thinker's Guide to Fallacies: The Art of Mental Trickery and Manipulation*. Dillon Beach, CA: Foundation for Critical Thinking Press.

———. (2009). *The Miniature Guide to Critical Thinking Concepts and Tools*. Dillon Beach, CA: Foundation for Critical Thinking Press.

———. (2009a). *The Thinker's Guide to the Art of Socratic Questioning*. Dillon Beach, CA: Foundation for Critical Thinking Press.

Pianta, R. (2007, Nov 6). Measure actual classroom teaching. *Education Week*, http://www.edweek.org/ew/articles/2007/11/07/11pianta.

Ravitch, D. (2009, September 16). Critical thinking? You need knowledge. *Boston Globe*, boston.com.

Redfield, C., & Rousseau, E. (1981). A meta-analysis of experimental research on teacher questioning behavior. *Review of Educational Research*, 51:237–45.

Reiman, A., & Thies-Sprinthall, L. (1998). *Mentoring and supervision for teacher development*. New York: Longman.

Rosenshine, B., & Meister, C. (1994). Reciprocal teaching: A review of the research. *Review of Educational Research*, 64, 479-530. 64(4), 479-530

Rowe, M. B. (1974). Wait-time and rewards as instructional variables, their influence on language, logic and fate control: Part 1: Wait-Time. *Journal of Research in Science Teaching*, 11:81–84.

———. (1986, January–February). Wait time: Slowing down may be a way of speeding up! *Journal of Teacher Education*, 37(1): 43–50.

Sadker, D., & Sadker, M. (1999). Questioning skills. In J. Cooper (Ed.), *Classroom Teaching Skills*, 6th ed., 101–46. Boston: Houghton Mifflin.

Sadker, M., & Sadker, D. (1994). *Failing at Fairness: How America's Schools Cheat Girls*. New York: Scribner.

———. (1997). *Teachers, Schools, and Society*. New York: McGraw-Hill.

Sawchuk, S. (2009, January 7). "21st century skills" focus shifts W. Va. teachers' role. *Education Week*, 28(15): 1, 12.

Sawchuk, S. (2009a, March 4). Backers of "21st-century skills" take flak. *Education Week*, 28(23): 1, 14.

Siegman, A. W., & Feldstein, S. (Eds.). (1987). *Nonverbal Behavior and Communication*. Hillsdale, NJ: Erlbaum.

Silvia, P. (2008). Interest—the curious emotion. *Current Directions in Psychological Science*, 17:57–60.

Slavin, R. E. (1997). *Educational Psychology: Theory and Practice*, 5th ed. Boston: Allyn & Bacon.

Snyder, D. (2009, June 11). Is the Socratic method dangerous? *ASCD Express*, 4(18) 1.

Sommers, C. H. (1996, June 12). Where the boys are. *Education Week*. Educationweek.org.

Sternberg, R. (1997). What does it mean to be smart? *Educational Leadership*, 54(6): 20–24.

———. (Summer, 2008). Assessing what matters. *Educational Leadership*, 65: 20–26.

Stevens, R. (1912). The question as a measure of efficiency in instruction: A critical study of classroom practice. *Teachers College Contributions to Education*, 48. New York: Teachers College.

Strauss, V. (2008, February 18). Relent questioning paves a deeper path. *Washington Post*, B02.

Stronge, J. (2002). *Qualities of Effective Teachers*. Alexandria, VA: Association for Supervision and Curriculum Development.

Suchman, R.J. (1962). *The Elementary School Training Program in Scientific Inquiry*. Report to the U.S. Office of Education, Project Title VII. Urbana: University of Illinois.

Tauber, R. (2007). *Classroom Management: Sound Theory and Effective Practice*, 4th ed. Portsmouth, NH: Praeger.

Tobias, S. (2008, August 22). Slowing speech eases a child's ability to listen. *Wichita Eagle*, Examiner.com/National.

Treffinger, D. (2008, Summer). Preparing creative and critical thinkers. *Educational Leadership* (65), Thinking skills NOW, Association for Supervision and Curriculum Development (online only).

Udelhofen, S. (2006). Writing essential questions. In *Curriculum Mapping Workshop: Integrating Assessment Data and Standards into Curriculum Maps, K-12*. Rye, NY: Center for Curriculum Mapping.

Vogler, K. (2008, Summer). Asking good questions. *Educational Leadership Online*.

Walsh, J. A., & Sattes, B. D. (2005). *Quality Questioning: Research-Based Practice to Engage Every Learner*. Thousand Oaks, CA: Corwin Press.

Wang, M., Haertel, G., & Walberg, H. (1993). Toward a knowledge base for school learning. *Review of Educational Research*, 63(3): 249–94.

Weiss, I., & Pasley, J. (2004). What is high-quality instruction? *Educational Leadership*, 61(5): 24–28.

White, R. T., & Tisher, R. P. (1986). Research on natural sciences. In M. C. Wittrock (Ed.), *Handbook of Research on Teaching*, 3rd ed. New York: Macmillan.

Wiggins, G. (1998). *Educative assessment: Designing assessments to inform and improve student performance*. San Francisco: Jossey-Bass.

Wiggins, G. (2005). *Educative assessment*, 2nd ed. Alexandria, VA: Association for Supervision and Curriculum Development.

Wilen, W. (2001). Exploring myths about teacher questioning in the social studies classroom. *Social Studies*, 92(1): 26–32.

Wilen, W., & Clegg, A. (1986). Effective questions and questioning: A research review. *Theory and Research in Social Education*, 14:153–61.

Willingham, D. (2009). *Why Don't Students Like School?* San Francisco: Jossey-Bass.

———. (2009a, Spring). Why don't students like school? Because the mind is not designed to think. *American Educator*, 33(1): 4–13.

Wolfe, P. (2001). Brain matters: *Translating research into classroom practice.* *Alexandria*, VA: Association for Supervision and Curriculum Development.

Wong, H. K. (1989). *How You Can Be a Successful Teacher*. Sunnyvale, CA: Harry Wong Tapes.

Woolfolk, A. (2008). *Educational psychology*, 10th ed. Boston: Pearson.

Wragg, E. C. (1993). *Primary Teaching Skills*. London: Routledge.

Wragg, E. C., & Brown, G. (2001). *Questioning in the Primary Schools*. London: Routledge.

Zhang, M., Lundeberg, M., McConnell, T., Koehler, M., & Eberhardt, J. (2010, January). Using questioning to facilitate discussion of science teaching problems in teacher professional development. *Interdisciplinary Journal of Problem-Based Learning*, 4(1): 57–82.

ABOUT THE AUTHOR

Marie Pagliaro is currently a professional development consultant. She was a full professor and director of the Teacher Education Division at Dominican College, chair of the Education Department at Marymount College, a supervisor of student teachers at Lehman College of the City University of New York, and chair of the Science Department and teacher of chemistry, general science, and mathematics in the Yonkers Public Schools. She received her PhD in curriculum and teaching from Fordham University.